SACHIN

SACHIN @50

Celebrating a Maestro

Concept and Curation
Boria Majumdar

Editorial Team
Kushan Sarkar
Arani Basu

Research
Debasis Sen
Trisha Ghosal

**SIMON &
SCHUSTER**

London · New York · Sydney · Toronto · New Delhi

First published in India by Simon & Schuster India, 2023

Copyright © Boria Majumdar, 2023

This book is copyright under the Berne Convention.

No reproduction without permission.

® and © 1997 Simon & Schuster, Inc. All rights reserved.

The right of Boria Majumdar to be identified as authors of this work has been
asserted by him in accordance with Section 57 of the Copyright Act 1957.

1 3 5 7 9 10 8 6 4 2

Simon & Schuster India
818, Indraprakash Building,
21, Barakhamba Road,
New Delhi 110001.

www.simonandschuster.co.in

Paperback ISBN: 978-93-92099-56-4
eBook ISBN: 978-93-92099-55-7

Typeset in India by SŪRYA, New Delhi
Printed and bound in India by Replika Press Pvt. Ltd.

FSC
www.fsc.org
MIX
Paper from
responsible sources
FSC® C016779

To every Sachin fan who has shouted
Sachinnn Sachinnn all their lives

CONTENTS

OPPONENTS

BEYOND CRICKET

FOURTH ESTATE

SACHINISTS

AJIT TENDULKAR, THE MENTOR

Editorial

Shakib Al Hasan was two when Sachin Tendulkar made his debut for India. When Tendulkar announced his retirement in 2013, Shakib was asked to write a newspaper column as tribute. He started it thus: 'I should have sought the permission of Sachin before attempting to write on him. He is the God of cricket, and how can I be expected to write about the God?'

Note that he didn't call him The Greatest or The Best Ever. But God. In a nutshell, that summed up what Tendulkar has had to live with for nearly three decades. And whether it was the woman running the bookshop at the Taj Coromandel in Chennai, a steward at St George's Park in Gqeberha (formerly Port Elizabeth) or a security officer in Lahore, they all wanted to know the same thing once they had seen you speak to him. 'What's he *really* like?' How can you even begin to answer that?

Think about it. Tendulkar has been a public figure for five different decades. More words have been written about him than there are people in Australia. He got standing ovation when he walked out to bat wherever he was in the world. But ask yourself this. How much do you know about the man behind the numbers, the character behind the prodigy who became one of the greatest there ever has been?

There are some echoes here of Joe DiMaggio, baseball's Yankee Clipper, who was even immortalised in song by Simon and Garfunkel. Many know of the 56-game hitting streak and the roses on Marilyn Monroe's grave till he died nearly two decades after she did, but few could answer the question: 'Where have you gone, Joe DiMaggio, a nation turns its lonely eyes to you?'

Like the baseball legend, Tendulkar is often as inscrutable as the Sphinx. When he speaks, he's invariably measured and thoughtful. But he makes sure he never says too much. As a result, there are no raging debates and even fewer controversies. There certainly isn't the public soap opera that was DiMaggio's tempestuous relationship with Monroe.

His family knows what he's like. A few friends do as well. The thing is, they're not going to talk to you. Omerta isn't just a Sicilian word. It sums up Tendulkar's inner circle. If you go blabbing to the tabloids or TV channels, you cease to be part of it.

For someone who grew up with unrelenting public scrutiny, Tendulkar has done remarkably well to avoid the pitfalls that snared many of his contemporaries. A wife and an older brother who guards his privacy as zealously as he does have helped, and so too did a management team that made him a household name without losing the mystique.

During his playing days, opportunities to do something 'normal' were a rarity. In India, visits to the cinema meant wigs and disguises. Going for a drive meant waiting for the wee hours and deserted roads. A family holiday involved travelling to places like Iceland, where there was little danger of anyone intruding on private time. It's a life that few can relate to, leave alone understand.

It wasn't always that way. As a teenager, who had returned from his first touring season, he loved to go around the city with friends in his new Maruti 800. In pre-liberalisation India, where trappings of success were very rare, it was almost unthinkable for an 18-year-old to own a car, however modest. But Tendulkar did, and he loved taking friends for a spin.

At Yorkshire in 1992, as the county's first overseas professional, he was given a sponsored car. Again, he loved zipping around in it, travelling here and there with Vinod Kambli, his great friend and batting partner from school days, who was playing some league cricket at the time. There were even impromptu meals at McDonald's, and when he left after a stint that helped remove many barriers at the most traditional of clubs, he spoke fondly of the experience.

It was the last normal summer of his life. As India opened up its economy and cricket became a big business—the board's first TV deal back in 1993 was worth \$40,000—

Tendulkar became the symbol of an aspirational generation. His appeal cut across age groups. Those in their 70s and 80s loved him because he was grounded and respectful. The younger lot loved him for his boundless enthusiasm and the flint-hard toughness that ensured no one could push him around. He was a new India that hadn't cast adrift its roots.

As your fame grows and the expectations grow ever higher, where does a man go to be himself? Childhood friends like Atul Ranade speak of a boy who used to be a bit of a playground bully, someone who aspired to emulate John McEnroe when most Indians preferred the calmness of Bjorn Borg. The boy-man shared McEnroe's rage to excel, but it was cloaked in the sort of composure that even Borg couldn't maintain for more than a decade.

His younger teammates loved him because he never pulled rank. Yuvraj Singh, who dedicated his World Cup-winning exploits to Tendulkar, and Harbhajan Singh won't hear a word against him, while Virender Sehwag always said he was one of the few players he'd pay to go and watch.

When Anil Kumble released a book of photographs over a decade ago, taken during the years he spent touring the world with the Indian team, some of the best ones were those taken during a team-bonding exercise under Gary Kirsten, India's coach between 2008 and 2011. One had Tendulkar wearing a long-haired wig and pretending to be Gabbar Singh, the iconic dacoit from the Hindi movie *Sholay*, which broke all box-office records when he was three years old. Ishant Sharma, gawky and towering over him, was Basanti, the object of his 'lustful' affections.

The serious side is not universally known, mainly because he has always believed that acts of kindness should be carried out away from the spotlight. The involvement with charity started primarily because of Annabel Mehta, his mother-in-law, who has been closely involved with Apnalaya. This organisation has worked with Mumbai's impoverished children for half a century. But while that remains close to his heart, he has since lent his support to many other worthwhile causes.

Few of those are closer to his heart than India's armed forces. After the terror attack in Mumbai in 2008, he appeared in a commercial for a bank with the compelling line: 'I play for India, now more than ever.' After a match-winning century against England in Chennai a few weeks later, he spoke of how it was the least he could do to lift national morale and of his boundless respect for the troops and commandos who had fought to bring the situation under control.

A few weeks after India's World Cup win in 2011, he was linked via satellite from a hotel room in Mumbai to the Paraplegic Rehabilitation Centre in Khadki (near Pune). Most soldiers there suffered spinal injuries during army operations and were paralysed below the waist or, in some cases, from the neck down.

During the chat, he promised them that he would visit

when he was next in Pune. So he did, too, a few weeks later, donating 1,000,000 Rupees simultaneously. During the two hours he spent with the soldiers, he watched them play basketball in wheelchairs. One of them was also a promising archer, and Tendulkar insisted that he would sponsor his trip to the world championships in Turin.

'Off the field, he's a different person,' says Sunandan Lele, a writer and friend who has accompanied him on several of these trips. 'He's wary of associating with too many charities because not everyone is straightforward, but whenever he's convinced about a cause, he does it wholeheartedly. For example, after meeting the army men, he was in tears of joy as much as anything. A lot of people send such folk money and presents. But to go and spend time with them...very few do what Sachin does. He constantly tells me to arrange such things and says he'll make time for it.'

After his retirement, Tendulkar was, for a time, part-owner of the Kerala Blasters football team in the Indian Super League (ISL). Despite having produced a couple of cricketers for India in recent decades, Kerala remains a football state where you're much more likely to come across a 30-foot cardboard cutout of Lionel Messi or Cristiano Ronaldo than one of Virat Kohli.

But even at the Nehru Stadium in Kochi, where he took his only two five-wicket hauls in international cricket, the Tendulkar factor was unmistakable. During the first season of the ISL in 2014, with the team struggling to sneak into the playoffs, Tendulkar attended their penultimate home game. Before kickoff, the mood was comparatively subdued. But when Tendulkar left the plush confines of the owners' box to take a lap of the stadium, the yellow-clad hordes were on their feet. The chants of 'Sach-in, Sach-in', India's cricket soundtrack for nearly a quarter century, were deafening, and you could see the joy and gratitude in Tendulkar's eyes as he soaked in the acclaim.

His journey from boy to man took place partly in the public eye, and that evolution can be traced partly through the endorsements that made him the nation's most recognisable figure. Some will have seen footage of his first TV interview as a 15-year-old. Tom Alter, of American descent but an institution in Indian cinema, asked the questions, and a gauche Tendulkar, who was clearly ill at ease expressing himself, tried to answer. You sensed that he would rather be 60 yards away, in the middle of the vast Wankhede Stadium.

A year later, he was seen with Kapil Dev, one of his heroes, in a commercial for a health drink. 'Boost is the secret of my energy' was the tagline, and again he came across as enthusiastic but stilted, a young man who preferred the camera to be on him only when he had a bat or ball in hand.

By the mid-1990s, the persona had started to change. He was noticeably more comfortable in front of a camera or microphone, and the commercials revealed a sense of fun that was worlds apart from the shy teenager. By then, he had also become a young man apart, the first to ink a multi-million-dollar deal in Indian sport. Long before the David Beckham phenomenon took over England, Tendulkar signed a deal with Worldtel in October 1995 that guaranteed him upward of $7 million over the next five years.

He has endorsed everything from shoes to cola to cars and the humble ballpoint pen. But there was always a line drawn in the sand. 'I will never advertise tobacco and alcohol,' he once said. 'I've received huge offers and turned them down because I feel I can't do that. They have tried to tempt me, but I think my family—and the principles I was raised with—have really helped me. It was never an option.'

As he travelled the world and became wiser about its ways, he indulged in some of his passions, taking a ride in a South African air-force jet—he loves speed of any kind, somehow appropriate for someone that Dennis Lillee turned down at the MRF Pace Foundation as a prospective fast bowler—and sampling the great cuisines of the world.

That love of food gave rise to Tendulkar's and Sachin's, two restaurants in Mumbai that he started in partnership with Sanjay Narang. Both featured plenty of autographed memorabilia and extensive menus that were affordable on a one-off basis for even his lower middle-class fans. What most visitors loved, though, were the personal touches. The menu told you which dishes were Tendulkar's favourites, and it's also worth noting that the cutlery had also been handpicked by the man whose eye for detail extended to much more than the opposition bowlers.

Many worship him for what he has achieved. There are a few that envy him. But the vast majority just struggle to comprehend how he has grown to middle age with such serenity. It's not been easy, this life of extremes. There have been times when it was easy to spot the yearning for normalcy. During the South African tour of 2006-07, when India played a warm-up game against a second-rung Kwa-Zulu Natal side at the small and picturesque Crusaders' Ground in Durban, Tendulkar was one of those rested.

On the first afternoon, at lunchtime, his son, Arjun, then just seven, went out to bat, left-handed, against some other kids. His father watched intently from outside the small pavilion, offering no advice but with a mixture of pride and apprehension—would the more ruthless perhaps judge the little boy?—on his face. It was the sort of mundane snapshot that life mainly had denied him.

The man and woman on the street connect to him for myriad reasons. It may have to do with having grown up with him. Or maybe it's just hard to think of anyone else who brings so many Indians together. One of Tendulkar's most celebrated fans was the late Lata Mangeshkar, India's nightingale. Of the thousands of songs she gave life to, one from Bollywood's 1960s golden age has the immortal lines: 'Tu Jahan Jahan Chalega, Mera Saaya Saath Hoga [Wherever you go, my shadow will follow you]'. It isn't only the hardcore cricket fan that feels that way about Tendulkar and his life and career quite unlike any other.

Anjali, the Best Half

ANJALI TENDULKAR

When you live with someone long enough, they become a part of you. To write about Sachin, therefore, isn't easy—because it is a reflection of myself as much as it is about him. We have known each other for 33 years now. Every day has been a celebration of our similarities and differences. We have gone through different stages of our partnership, like every couple—courtship, marriage, becoming parents, and to now seeing our children become adults and carve out their own lives.

We come from very different cultural backgrounds. Yet, we have been brought up with the same value systems. Both of us believe in according every person's dignity and respect. What is praiseworthy about Sachin is that despite all the fame and adulation, he still treats everyone equally. Irrespective of someone's position in society, he treats everyone the same. Whoever comes to our home is our guest—and they will be treated with the same warmth. Money, power and success are immaterial; what comes foremost is that every person is a unique human being who deserves respect. Sachin and I feel very strongly about this, which we have tried to pass on to our children as well.

We have differences as well. For example, both of us love gadgets. But I would go through the operations manual before I start operating one, whereas Sachin would be more hands-on, and he would work his way through the device and figure it out by using it.

We have both supported each other in our personal and professional lives. When Sachin played for India, there would be phases when I realized he needed to be given the space required. Likewise, he has been a very supportive partner. Many people have asked me what I have planned for Sachin's 50th birthday. We have been very private people— so this birthday will be no different. It'll be something with very close friends and family.

Teammates

SOURAV GANGULY

Sachin is and will always remain a special person. And it was an absolute pleasure to have him and his family with us for my 50th birthday celebrations in London in July 2022. It was much like old times. We had a lot of food together and just chatted. Went back in time to the good old days. To the many moments, we have spent together. To the many successes and failures, we shared together. What was fantastic was the presence of a grown-up Sara, who I had seen as an infant in New Zealand in 1997. I had taken our daughters out for dinner, and it was such a heartwarming sight to see the two beautiful ladies converse. In 1997 Sara was finding it hard to adjust to the time zone in New Zealand. It was natural for an infant. And I remember Anjali sitting in the hotel lobby at night with baby Sara on her lap to try and allow Sachin some sleep, for we had a game the next day. Dona and I would take turns to give her a break, and to see the same Sara grow up into such a beautiful, intelligent girl is an absolute delight. Anjali was also there for my 50th, which made the whole experience special. Some relationships just mean a lot to you. My bond with Sachin is one such.

Sachin and I go back a really long way. The first time I met Sachin was at an under-14 camp in Indore. We were 13, Sachin eight months younger, and we were there at the camp conducted by Vasu Paranjpe under the aegis of the Madhya Pradesh Cricket Association. Sanjay Jagdale was instrumental in putting the camp together. I first noticed that the curly-haired boy from Bombay just loved to bat. He was the first at the nets and just kept batting. Such was his passion and intensity that Vasu had to eventually pull him out on occasions. Sachin would just bat, bat and bat. At the camp, everyone talked about him, and it was apparent that he was blessed with exceptional talent. He would hold the bat lower than the norm; this would mean he'd not feel the pressure of his heavy bat. He already had all the shots in the book and timed the ball beautifully.

After that first meeting, Sachin had catapulted himself into the national reckoning within a couple of years. He had already scored hundreds at the Ranji and Irani trophies before he was 17. So it wasn't a surprise that at 16, he was picked for the Indian tour to Pakistan in 1989. I did not watch many of his knocks in Pakistan as I was touring with the Bengal team. However, I watched the one match where he took apart Abdul Qadir. It was a rain-curtailed ODI reduced to a 20-over-a-side exhibition contest. However, when it is an India versus Pakistan match, it can never be not seriously competitive. When Sachin came out to bat, the asking rate had gone well over 10 an over, and India needed a miracle. That nearly happened, thanks to Sachin. He went ballistic and scored 53 of 18 balls, and in the process, hit four sixes to Qadir to all corners of the ground. It was incredible hitting. Once again, it was an announcement to the broader cricket world that he was special. Eventually, India lost by a meagre four runs.

We again met during India's tour to Australia in 1992. I was part of the team but wasn't expected to play the Tests, while Sachin gradually established himself as the team's premier batsman. Importantly, we were roommates during this tour, and I remember him in Sydney the night before he went on to get his first century in Australia. India was down 0-2, and we needed to play well in Sydney to regain confidence. Sachin just refused to sleep that night. I remember telling him that if he was to play the next day, he desperately needed to sleep. He said he couldn't and started telling me where he would hit McDermott and the others! By midnight I was asleep, leaving him to his devices. The next day he said to me that he was starved of sleep and that he'd nap on the dining table in the team dressing room at the SCG. He asked me to wake him up at the fall of the next wicket. Sachin was to bat at number six, and I woke him up when Azhar got out. He said he was refreshed now that he'd had some sleep. It was odd how he could sleep on a dining table! He played a terrific innings of 148, not out, and I believe we should have won the Sydney Test.

However, his best of the series was yet to come. It came in Perth in what was the world's fastest wicket. The WACA pitch is now slower than in 1992, and it was undoubtedly one of the hardest wickets to bat on. Sachin's height made it more challenging to negotiate the excessive bounce, for it was impossible for a short man to play shots in front of the wicket. I can say it was the best innings of his career. To score a hundred on that wicket against the Australian bowling attack was simply sensational. Most of our other batsmen weren't even able to get bat on ball, and here was an 18-year-old putting together a batting master class.

After the Australia tour, I was dropped from the Indian team, and it was in 1996 that Sachin and I again shared the dressing room in England. I batted well in the tour games leading up to the tests, and he came up to me one day to say my opportunity would come soon. I hadn't played the first Test where he got a hundred. However, we lost the match at Edgbaston and conceded a 0–1 lead to England. I got my chance in the Second Test. I was to bat at three, while Sachin was to bat at four. We were not out overnight in our first partnership, and he kept telling me to play straight and get behind the line of the ball. The following day, he got out to a peach from Chris Lewis while I managed to get to a century. At tea, when I returned to the dressing room, my bat started to make a creaky sound due to the pounding it had taken. Sachin came up to me and said that I should just relax as I had to bat post tea, and he would tape my bat up. He did so, and I could keep playing with it through the innings. At the end of the day, he said it was just a start, and I should not give it away, and I had a long Test career ahead of me and should make the most of my talent.

We played a tour game between the second and third Tests at Hampshire in which I batted with one of Sachin's bats because mine was broken. Our bats were of the same weight, and I remember walking up to him to ask if I could borrow a bat of his. He was accommodating as usual, and I got a hundred once again. Unfortunately, most of the other teammates were very senior, so I couldn't ask them for their bats. Sachin and I had been friends for nearly a decade, which was par for the course.

In the next Test at Trent Bridge, we both got hundreds. I remember in one particular session before lunch, he was finding it extremely difficult to negotiate the swing. He was beaten several times but, being a true great, was still not out on 30 or so at lunch. I was unbeaten at 44 when we went back for the breather. Watching from the other end, I felt Sachin was going too hard at the ball when he could have just timed the deliveries. Over lunch, I told him hushedly where he was going wrong. Post lunch, he was a different batsman. In fact, he reached his hundred before me, and Geoffrey Boycott said on commentary that he wondered what Sachin had for lunch, for he had come out a completely different batsman.

He is the greatest cricketer I have ever seen. I haven't

seen Bradman, but he is as close to perfection as you can get. His insatiable hunger and incredible talent made him an absolute genius. When people say things about him, I point to them the 100 international hundreds. Can you imagine the hunger and motivation of a player who has achieved that? The difference between Sachin and a really good player is that the latter, if he scores a hundred in the first innings and has once again scored a fifty in the second, will, in all likelihood, play one loose shot after that. It happened to us all. Sachin, however, will leave nothing to chance and will get the second innings hundred as well. That's why I always say that Lara was great and Ponting was brilliant, but Sachin, without hesitation, is the greatest.

I will not be exaggerating if I say that, barring Sachin; no one knows his game better than I do. In fact, on occasions, I could read his mind with consummate ease. If he shuffled across to the off side with his feet at an angle, I could sense that he was lining himself up to go over square leg. In fact, it once happened that he was trying to hit Shaun Pollock over square leg and was moving towards his off stumps to do so. The pitch did not offer enough pace for the shot, and it was apparent that the wily Pollock wouldn't bowl him a short one. I went up to him and told him as much, and he soon changed his plan of attack.

Of course, he would do the same to me and often cautioned me from playing too many shots on the off side. Having batted for years together, we could read each other's minds, making batting together enjoyable.

While I can keep going on and on about the best batsman I have seen and played with, I will restrict myself to talking about one more incident for the paucity of space. This is about the 2003 World Cup in South Africa. It was a tournament where we played some of our best cricket ever, and Sachin was in imperious form right through.

Before the tournament, there was a debate over his batting position. I felt he should bat at number four and guide the middle order. Needless to say, I was wrong. We had a meeting in South Africa between John Wright, Anil Kumble, Sachin and myself, and Anil suggested that he open the batting for us. I asked Sachin what he wanted to do, and he preferred to bat at the top of the order. I had never imposed my wish on my teammates and agreed to the proposition. The rest, as they say, is history. Sachin tore into opposition bowling attacks and guided us to the final. And this included playing one of his best knocks ever against Pakistan at Centurion on 1 March 2003.

Pakistan had scored a challenging 273 batting first. While walking out at mid-innings, I asked Sachin if we should have a team talk. He was clear we shouldn't. He said we were already playing very well, and there was no need to disturb the momentum. Discussion would only end up confusing the boys. So I dropped the idea and left it to him to go out and play his game. Needless to say, he did. We hit 60 in the first five overs, and soon it was all over for Pakistan. Sachin again did it for us with an innings of the highest calibre. It was the tournament's most high-pressure encounter, and he delivered when it mattered the most.

While wishing him a very happy 50th birthday, it is time I say it for one final time. He is the best I have seen and will ever see. No batsman in the next decade and more can score 100 international hundreds. Well done, my friend. And a very happy birthday.

HARBHAJAN SINGH

When I got scared seeing an angry Sachin

I was 13 when I first got a glimpse of Sachin Tendulkar but sadly, from a height of at least 30 feet and an 80-metre distance.

Indian and Sri Lankan teams were engaged in one among its innumerable bilateral ODIs back in 1993–94. Little did I know then that I would be a fixture of many such contests in the future. That day, I was one of the designated ball boys who had been summoned from local academies. But a problem arose, and there were way too many ball boys at the boundary line.

So one of the officials told me to climb up the iron stairs and help the scorers run the Manual scoreboard. So even when India fielded, Sachin mostly stood in the inner circle. So I was dejected. But I did watch Vinod (Kambli) closely standing near the boundary line.

But I did enjoy one thing. Sachin scored quite a few runs,

and it was fun helping the scorer change the digit plates. However, once the match ended, those were pre-ACU days, and everyone tried entering the dressing room. Police could hardly control it as many organisers were trying to jostle for photos. I, the little sardar, climbed down the scoreboard and, with my pencil-thin frame, could manoeuvre easily among the big-bodied sardars and managed to sneak into the dressing room.

I saw Sachin for the first time; he was barely 20 and looked baby-faced. After that, I went back home and bragged about seeing Sachin to anyone who would listen. The first proper introduction to Sachin happened around three years later, in 1997, when I had already made a name in junior cricket as the guy who could bowl the doosra. I was summoned to India nets in Mohali before a Test match against Sri Lanka.

I bowled for a few days and for hours to all the India batters—Sachin, Rahul, and Dada. I was awestruck when I first saw Sachin at the other end of 22 yards. I was spellbound, as any fan would be. But there were no nerves while bowling, and he did tell me, 'Aur mehnaat karna'.

I was indeed in a daze.

In a year, I was already playing for India in a Test match with Sachin Tendulkar as my teammate. But our friendship grew deeper after my breakthrough series against Australia in 2001. There were two things that I remember after the Kolkata hat-trick. First, Paaji came up to me and said: 'Bol

Bhajji kya chahiye tujhe (Tell me, Bhajji, what do you want?)'
I hesitantly said, 'Paaji, I love your Adidas bowling spikes.
Can you get me a pair?' Sachin laughed and said, 'Bas itni
si baat (That's it. That's all you want?)?' Within a week,
an Adidas representative came with a couple of expensive
bowling spikes, which I used for the next three years.

The other thing was more important in the context of
my development. After the Chennai Test against Australia,
which we won and clinched the series, Sachin, I remember,
pulled a chair and sat beside me long after the Test got over.
'Bhajju, have you seen a racehorse? It doesn't look sideways.
It doesn't have peripheral vision. It looks straight, and eyes
are transfixed on the target. You have to be that. You cannot
be distracted by the stardom which you have attained now.
You will have too many friends and well-wishers around
you. You need to know who are your real friends and be
careful whom you befriend,' Sachin had told me back then.

The other thing I learnt was humility. The more Sachin
achieved on the field, the more humble he became of it.
But if you thought Sachin Tendulkar never got angry, think
twice. Yours truly once got his rough end of the stick during
a tour of Australia in 1999.

It was in one of the tour matches, and I played that game
as I didn't get a chance in the Test matches. I was stationed
at the boundary, and a few pretty girls were sitting near the
boundary. For a 20-year-old who had just started touring
and was on his first trip to Australia, stealing a few furtive

glances and exchanging smiles I thought were par for the course.

Now because of my inattentiveness, I was late in anticipating a few shots that came towards the boundary. But things got worse when I got caught busy ogling, and I didn't hear Sachin shouting from mid-on, as he wanted a field change. Instead, before I realised it, he was standing beside me, visibly angry.

'Bhajji, please know one thing. You have seen my good side, but if I want, I can be rude, and you wouldn't like to see that side of me, you better concentrate.' I wanted to run for cover as I started what you can call 'shitting bricks'. For the rest of the fielding session, I didn't even dare to turn and look back towards the gallery.

Sachin is a very competitive person and hates losing games, even on PlayStation. So once I, along with Yuvi (Yuvraj Singh), Ashu (Ashish Nehra), Zak (Zaheer Khan) and Ajit (Agarkar), decided we had to beat him in a Go-karting simulator game which we played in New Zealand during the tour of 2002. So now I was entrusted with regularly colliding with Sachin's car.

As I started to deliberately hit his 'car' from the side, he got irritated. 'Sardar ji, what exactly are you doing. Why are you colliding with me?' I mumbled, 'Sorry, Paaji not able to control the car.'

I have countless memories with Sachin, both on and off the field. The kind of support I got post the infamous

Monkey Gate was incredible. He defended me stoutly in front of the match referee and the CA panel. Sachin stood by me like a rock during those dark days when I was at my lowest ebb.

I must have done something right in my life that I got to grace the field alongside Sachin Tendulkar.

AJINKYA RAHANE

Sachin Tendulkar has been a role model for every Indian cricketer. And none of us needs to say how good he was. He was the best ever, and that's known to one and all. A hundred international hundreds and there should be no further talk about how good a batsman he was. For someone growing up in Mumbai and aspiring to play the sport, he was a God. We all wanted to be like him. Bat like him. Play strokes like him. Dominate bowling attacks like him. Score runs all across the world like him.

In this piece, I will refrain from commenting on how good Sachin Paaji was. But, as I said, it's known to one and all. So instead, I'd like to speak about two incidents where Sachin Paaji impacted my life. The first took place in 2013 on the day of Paaji's retirement. And the second was in December 2020, when I had the honour of captaining India at the MCG when we were 0–1 down and had lost the Adelaide Test getting bowled out for 36.

Soon after, the match against the West Indies ended

on 16 November 2013 at the Wankhede, and Paaji was back alone in the changing room, having completed his retirement speech. Each one of us felt the emotions. At Wankhede, there are three rooms adjacent to each other, of which the first is the big change room, then there is a small space where Paaji was sitting, and the third is the physio's room. We had decided to give Paaji some space, and I was astonished when he called me over. We always sought Paaji out for advice, but here it was the other way around. It was Sachin Paaji who had called me.

I was the 12th man in that match and had yet to really get my chances in the preceding two years. And yet I had trained the hardest possible and had always kept myself prepared to grab the first opportunity that came my way. Paaji had seen me from very close and had this to say.

'I have known you for years and have seen how much you love the game. You have been the perfect devotee and have served cricket with all the dedication and commitment over the last few years. You might feel hard done by what has happened so far in your career, but you should continue to be the way you are. You played the last Test match of the series against Australia in March 2013; Rohit has come up and grabbed your spot on the back of a fantastic one-day double hundred against Australia. With two consecutive hundreds, Rohit made the spot his own, at least for a while, and you were left to wait for your turn. It wasn't easy on you. It is always challenging to sit out and keep oneself motivated. But you will get your chance, and you should grab it with both hands once you do. For the moment, you may feel it is a cruel game, but I am certain the game will take care of you in the future if you continue to serve it the way you have always done.'

Paaji said he was very pleased with my attitude and commitment to the game and commended me for it. I was stunned. For him to call me on a day like this and spend 15 minutes speaking to me was unthinkable. While the whole world was thinking about him, he talked to me and prepared me for the future. If I was ever in need of motivation, I had it in front of me. I can't describe in words what that conversation meant to me. Each time I have faced adversity, I have returned to that conversation with Sachin Paaji and never changed my attitude or commitment to the game. As long as I play the sport, I will stay committed to cricket the same way I was in 2013.

The second incident I want to share happened in December 2020 when I was asked to captain India at the MCG. We were down 0–1 in the series and had been bowled out for 36 in Adelaide. It was the worst we had played as a team, and with Virat returning to India for personal reasons, I was asked to take over the reins in the most challenging circumstances. As skipper, I had to lead from the front. For a young team to take heart, the captain had to score. And that's when my thoughts went back to Paaji. He scored a hundred at the MCG in 1999, and I still rate it as one of his best knocks. He dominated the Australian attack, and I decided to watch the video of that knock multiple times before I went out to bat. In fact, I remember seeing the innings five or six times before walking out, and it helped me immensely. I went on to score a hundred at the MCG in a Boxing Day Test, and more importantly, we won the Test match and levelled the series. After that, we went on to win the series after a spectacular effort in Brisbane, and it will forever rank as the best series win of my career. In a significant way, Paaji was with me in this victory. Yet again, I sought inspiration from his innings and returned to the conversation at the Wankhede. It was about commitment, attitude, and my approach to the game as captain of India.

As Paaji turns 50, may I say to him that his words have never left me and will never. I will always try to stay true to the sport and honour his faith in me. And he will always remain a role model for us all in India. Happy birthday Sachin Paaji.

RAVICHANDRAN ASHWIN

Sachin was not just a cricketer. He was much more. He was a symbol of hope. A reminder that we Indians were capable of taking on the world. Each time he played Australia in the 1990s, and Australia was the best cricketing nation in the world then, he raised his game. It was as if it came naturally to him. He launched into Australian attacks, including the likes of Shane Warne in India, and got the better of them in Sharjah. And each time he did so, young Indians like us would start to dream with him. We believed it was possible. That we could take on the best in the world and win. Here was someone who was doing it time and again, day in and day out.

If you really want to understand the significance of Sachin Tendulkar in our lives, you need to go beyond the cricket field. It is not just about the runs scored or the 100 hundreds. Staggering as the statistics are, there is more to the Sachin phenomenon than just numbers. Each hundred meant our hope turned a little more resolute. Each of us would believe in our abilities a little more. Our self-confidence received a boost each time Sachin did something extraordinary. And it happened with remarkable regularity for a good two decades.

We are a young country and a nation that is still growing. Sachin was part of this growth story. He was the voice young India needed to speak out to the world in the 1990s. Rahul Dravid, Sourav Ganguly and VVS Laxman joined him later, making India a real force to reckon with in cricket. Sachin led this charge by being the embodiment of excellence, which in a way, defined India's growth story.

I played some of my cricket with Sachin, and the high point has to be the 2011 World Cup. He had waited 22 years for the world title, yet again, it defined him. He had never given up hope and was putting in the hardest possible effort to achieve his dream. He wanted to be the best in the world, and nothing else would suffice. That was him. All hard work and self-belief, and single-minded pursuit of excellence. He inspired me greatly in trying to become the cricketer I am. To try and excel each time I stepped onto the field wearing the India jersey. Be the best version of myself against the best of opponents.

It was fitting that we dedicated the 2011 World Cup triumph to him. He was the kind of glue which had galvanized the nation. Each time he would walk out to bat, it was as if all of India was doing the same with him. He shaped our understanding of what Indians can achieve. And that's his real legacy. Hope. Giving us all hope each day he played the sport. And we are forever grateful to him for this.

DEEP DASGUPTA

Watching a 'scientist' at play

It was my first tour with the Indian team. We were in South Africa in 2001 when I first got the experience of the 'scientist' in Sachin Tendulkar. During training on the eve of a Test match, he called me and asked me to take some throws from him. It seemed a routine drill until he asked, 'Deep, how was the last throw?' I responded: 'It was a good throw. Certainly, better than the rest of the throws.'

What followed blew my mind. 'Deep, if I keep the seam of the ball parallel to the ground and throw, I got a good lift and carry, the ball travels faster, and I need to put in less effort,' he responded.

Sachin Tendulkar's mind is always ticking, and he is constantly studying different elements of the game. That was on display in Australia in 2003–04 when he played that memorable knock of 241 not out in the final Test in Sydney. Everyone knows he was struggling on that tour and that he had eschewed the cover drive.

When he finished the innings and returned to the dressing room, he looked at me and asked: '*Dekha, kya kiya?* (Did you see what I did?)' And then he said: 'I didn't play a single cover drive.' I was astounded. That was his genius.

He didn't bat in the nets during the tour. He would just take throwdowns and do some knocking. Then, he got into match mode on the eve of the matches. He would literally seclude himself and stay in his room. He worked on his bat and other things. He would be visualizing himself batting already. But it's his planning that is astounding.

If you observe closely, he always went in with a plan on how he wanted to bat on a particular day. Sometimes he would decide that if anything is fractionally short, he will go after them. Some days he would look to play more on the front foot, and on some other days, he will shuffle back and across. The greatest thing about that innings in Sydney was that even if he took out the cover drive—the most heavy-scoring shot for any batter—the runs kept flowing at his usual rate. Every batter has an attacking game or a defensive game. Even if he struggled, he never let that impact the scoreboard.

Another incident comes to my mind when we talk about his scientific bent of mind. We were in West Indies. We all know about his fascination with cars. At the dinner table, he asked if I was interested in cars. I just said yes, and then he took the discussion to a new level. He started talking about parts, micro parts and technologies used in different cars. He knew the minutest of detail about cars. And this was the pre-smartphone and pre-easy-internet-access days. He gathered all that knowledge just by speaking to actual car experts.

There's another example of his attention to detail. Of course, his fondness for music is also well-known. But he designed a room in his house in such a way (in terms of furniture and aesthetics) that would allow you to enjoy music in its truest form.

And how can I forget the Ranji Trophy final when I captained Bengal against Mumbai at Wankhede stadium in 2006–07. We were bowling first on Day One on a damp pitch that aided spongy disconcerted bounce and movement. We got two wickets early, and Sachin Tendulkar came to take strike.

We had a raw Ashok Dinda steaming in. Dinda liked to get under the skin of batters. One ball took off from a length, hit Sachin on his forearm and went past short leg. He didn't even flinch. Dinda went up to him and gave him a stare. I rushed from behind the stumps and had to scold Dinda away back to his run-up. We had decided we would not nudge Tendulkar, but Dinda did the exact opposite. Slowly, Sachin started unfurling his shots. It seemed he decided to play different shots to deliveries from the same line and length. The drives on the rise and the pulls and cuts were ferocious. Needless to say, he brought up his century at a rapid rate.

Sachin Tendulkar is a genius, and it came from his observing and learning every minute thing.

CHANDRAKANT PANDIT

**What happened when seniors tried to run out a
12-year-old teammate**

Ramakant Achrekar had that aura that even when you
became an established first-class cricketer, his word was
cast in stone. However, there is one specific incident from
nearly 38 years back, which, to date, I haven't been able to
forget. Obviously, who else but Sachin Tendulkar was the
protagonist.

It was 1985, and I had already played for Mumbai and
was about to come into the national reckoning. It was just
after India's Benson & Hedges triumph in 1985, and the
50-over game was catching up fast. I was the Kamat Club's
captain, which was run by our Sir (Achrekar). We had a
full-fledged match against New Hind Club at the Matunga
Gymkhana ground.

Now, sir came in the morning and instructed me,
'Chandu, you need to play Sachin, and he should get to bat

in the top five. No way you are going to bench him.' Well,
I wasn't convinced that someone that young, just about 12
years old, could field for 50 overs. Also, it was a senior team's
match, and a few seniors and I were convinced that Sachin's
shots won't have that power.

And trust me, even Achrekar sir knew that he needed
to generate more power. Since we failed to convince sir,
three to four of us decided that whoever gets the first
opportunity should run him out as we would need quick
runs. Accordingly, when Sachin batted, on my instructions,
one of our senior guys tried at least twice to deliberately run
him out by calling him for non-existent singles.

Somehow the little one managed to avoid getting out
and returned to the crease. But Sachin realised that we
were trying to run him out, and what he did next was
unimaginable. There was a straightforward single, and he
called the other guy and ran him out. Of course, there was
momentary anger for me, but his cricketing smarts and
sharp mind have stayed with me all these years.

Another regular incident that stayed with me was his
eagerness to continue batting at the nets for hours, and he
didn't mind asking seniors when they would finish their
stint. This was 1986, and I had just made my India debut.
During the off-season, I was at Shivaji Park to practice at sir's
nets. So now, whenever I would go out to bat, I would find
Sachin padding up and standing right behind the nets. After
every 20 minutes, he would ask, 'Tera ho gaya kya (Are you

done?)? Main jaaon (Should I go?)?' I would look at him and wonder, 'Yeh kya cheez hai (Who is this guy?)?' I would say curtly, 'Be quiet and let me bat.' But after 10 more minutes, again, the same query, 'Are you done?'

Now for an established Mumbai player who had already played for India, all these things didn't matter. All he wanted was to bat, and he didn't care if it was a senior player. Of course, at that time, I was a young player, but I had that instinct to understand which guy was going in the right direction.

He was about 13 and already on the right track.

Achrekar sir's methods also helped him a lot. By the time Sachin entered the Ranji arena, he had played countless official and unofficial senior-level club games in Mumbai. He was tremendously cricket fit, playing five simultaneous matches at the Azad, Cross and Oval maiden. Such was Achrekar sir's respect in the Mumbai maidan that he would take any of us, whether it was me, Praveen (Amre), Sachin or Ajit (Agarkar), and no one would refuse us matches on his request.

We would ride on his scooter after school and hop around maidans to play games. That's how Sachin developed his tremendous game awareness. And as I spoke about his passion as 13-year-old who wanted to bat for hours, I saw that in a 36-year-old at the business end of his career when I was the Director of MCA's cricket academy. It was before one tour of Sri Lanka he would come every day to bat for hours. But what stuck with me was his continuous preparation against the yorker.

He would bat for two hours against the yorker, and once satisfied, he would proceed with normal nets. I asked him one day, and his answer was, 'This guy Lasith Malinga bowls lethal yorkers, and I need to prepare well.' Here was the world's best batter with 150 plus Tests, yet the hunger to stand up to new challenges was just like any 20-year-old.

Sachin, for me, will remain the epitome of passion.

VIJAY DAHIYA

When 2 not out got me space in the newspaper

It takes work to idolize someone who is your age. What was I doing when I was only 16 years old? I was playing cricket but trying to make a mark in the Delhi age group cricket through the ranks.

So when I knew I might get to meet Sachin Tendulkar during a BCCI Conditioning Camp in Chennai before the Champions Trophy in Nairobi in 2000, I was also a 27-year-old like the legend himself. The only difference was that he played Test cricket at 16, and I, all these years, stood in front of his posters, secretly harbouring hopes of meeting him once.

Let me make it very clear. I don't belong to Sachin's close friend circle, but having had the honour of playing a couple of Tests and 19 ODIs allowed me the privilege of sharing the dressing room with Sachin for some time, something that will be a part of my treasure trove.

Now back to the Chennai camp. The first day we got on the bus and on our way to Chepauk for the training session, I had rehearsed in my mind at least 50 times what could be the best way to introduce myself. But, till then, I hadn't had a chance to meet him personally.

As a new entrant, I was sitting at the back of the team bus, and it was Sachin who came up to us, all newcomers. 'Hi, I am Sachin,' he introduced himself with utmost humility. Why does he need an introduction? Do I tell him that despite being his contemporary in terms of age, I used to get his posters to adorn the walls of my room? One of the last memories I have of Sachin, the player, is his short but impactful innings against Australia at Nairobi.

Yes, Yuvi (Yuvraj Singh) announced his arrival in that game against Australia, but Sachin's 30-odd (38) set the tone and how he took on Glenn McGrath and Brett Lee. He made a quick technical switch while playing that innings. He decided to widen his stance, and thus the distance between his two feet increased considerably.

When you have a narrower stance, it helps in the quick shuffling of back and across movement for horizontal bat shots. But Sachin decided that to tackle the pace and bounce generated by McGrath, Lee and Jason Gillespie, he won't transfer his weight on the backfoot and also with a considerably lower backlift. There is another thing that I remember from that game. Sachin was hit flush on the 'box' (abdomen guard).

Trust me, sitting in the dressing room, I freaked out as it was a good 140 clicks, and this man didn't even flinch, leave aside even rubbing the part. He didn't want the Aussies to feel that he was in any pain or discomfort whatsoever. No inch given, and trust me when I say that any other person might have needed a bit of help from physio.

Because once Sachin was dismissed and he was back in the dressing room, he went to the washroom and winced and howled in pain, it was that bad, but till he was at the crease, he didn't want to show it hurt.

My second and last Test match in 2000 was memorable as Sachin scored a double hundred against Zimbabwe in Nagpur at the Old ground. In fact, I was at the non-striker's end we declared the innings. Well, since we were both returning to the pavilion, my photo was also published prominently in the next day's paper despite scoring only 2 not out.

I remember joking, 'Apne 200 banaya aur maine 2 lekin picture same aaya (You made 200 and I made 2 but we are in the same frame together!).'

His simplicity makes him the legend he is. He has time for everyone and meets with so much warmth during the post-match chit-chat after IPL games.

I have played with Sachin Tendulkar, and I have tales for my grandkids.

GURSHARAN SINGH

Tale of a broken finger

The Irani Cup match between Rest of India and Ranji Trophy Champions Delhi just before the 1989 tour of Pakistan was also supposed to be my match. After all, the vice-captain of the Rest of India team in those days would be in the national reckoning after a good Ranji Trophy season.

Glad it wasn't my match after all. I am even more proud that I was one of the brief but significant co-passenger in Sachin Tendulkar's illustrious cricketing journey. That co-passenger with whom you share your seat for a couple of stations but share such warmth that the sweet aftertaste remains for a lifetime.

This is Sachin Tendulkar's story and not mine. So it was never about whether I would remember Sachin or not. It was about whether Sachin remembers me in his journey. I know he does.

I have had 14 first-class hundreds and a career-best of

298 in a Ranji game, but the 5 not out that I made on the fifth day of that Irani Cup match remains one of the highlights of my career. I had helped Sachin get that hundred which paved his way for national selection for that tour of Pakistan.

Believe me, the kind of talent Sachin was, had he scored even 80 and not a hundred, he would have gone, but Mumbai players of that era were made of different mettle.

The 1989 Delhi team is one of the best in the history of the Ranji Trophy. Barring Raman Lamba and Manoj Prabhakar, everyone played that game. There was Bhasi (K.P. Bhaskar), Bantoo (Singh), Bhaiyoo (Kirti Azad), Manu (Nayar), and Rajiv (Vinayak) in the batting lineup.

Two quick bowlers, Vivek (Razdan) and Atul (Wassan), were in India reckoning. Sanjeev (Sharma) was already playing for India, and Manni (Maninder Singh) was a star. And the peerless Maddi Paa was playing his last first-class game.

The Wankhede track, I remember, was perfect for batting, but in that first innings, I was timing the ball well, but when I was in my 20s, Sanjeev bowled a short ball, and I wanted to hook it. Sanjeev's deliveries weren't that quick, but his short ball was deceptive. I couldn't connect it, and it hit the middle finger of my right hand.

These kinds of fractures you don't realise instantly as I carried on batting before Atul got me leg before of an inside edge. In his syndicated column, I remember Sunny bhai (Gavaskar) had written, 'entire Wankhede heard the inside edge except for the umpire'.

It was the third day of the match, and an X-ray confirmed I had a fracture, and my finger was heavily taped. Sunny bhai presented one of his SG gloves with double padding on the middle fingers.

I remember Delhi had set us a target of 500 plus (555), and the fifth day was a mere formality. But then the baby-faced genius wasn't there to add numbers. I was in my track pants and coloured shirt sitting in the dressing room and knowing that I won't bat and also a chance of selection was gone with my injury. But then I saw a 16-year-old with such poise and balance that I hadn't seen before.

In '89, trust me, Atul was quick enough for any other 16-year-old, but his drives off him on the rise is something I remember whenever I close my eyes. Of course, we had all come up the ranks, but I hadn't ever seen such power and punch in a teenager's shot before.

And Manni was the toughest bowler on the final day as he was getting a lot of turn and a few that kept low. Sachin was in his 60s when the eighth wicket fell. Suddenly Raj bhai (Raj Singh Dungarpur) came up to me and said, 'Gush pad up. You need to go out after the next wicket.'

Anyone with a hairline fracture would know you can't even raise your finger; mine was a broken bone. 'Raj bhai, I can't even raise my hand, and you are asking me to bat,' I pleaded.

One thing about the late Raj Singh Dungarpur was that he didn't beat around the bush. Instead, he came straight to the point.

'Look, Sachin has scored a century on Ranji and Duleep Trophy debut, and I would like him to score a hundred in Irani Cup. After that, no one will question his selection for the Pakistan tour. So you need to give him company,' Raj bhai bluntly told me.

At the end of the day, sardars aren't known to back out. So at 209 for 9, in walked an injured Gursharan Singh! In those days, I loved how Sachin interacted with us. He was very respectful but never overawed. 'Gush, tu khel payegaa naa,' the squeaky childish voice enquired as I walked up to join him in the middle.

'Sachin tu bindaas khel. Aaj toh tera century karwake hi niklunga,' I told him. But what he told me next was something I wouldn't forget ever.

'Gush, let me handle Manni as he gets the ball to turn away. You can only hold the bat with one hand. So you should play Kirti as the ball will come in, and you can play it with one hand,' Sachin told me. In our 36-run stand, I scored only five.

Sachin understood that playing Manni standing on the crease would be difficult. So the next half an hour was an exhibition of how to use feet against a spinner on top of his game till then.

The innings was terminated when Sachin hit the boundary to reach a hundred. I did again interact with Sachin on our tour of New Zealand, my first and last with the national team. The 88 at Hamilton was sheer class, and I saw him in tears when he missed that hundred.

He is a great player but an even better human being.

He told me, 'Gush, jaabhi tera benefit match hoga, main aayega khel ne.' He did keep his word, and in 2005, he came for my benefit game along with Rahul Dravid and Sourav Ganguly. He came by a morning flight, and despite the steady drizzle, he insisted we play a game.

'Aaj Gush ka din hai. Aaj khelenge.' He also gifted me a bat to auction, fetching me a decent amount.

I would remain a footnote in Sachin's illustrious journey. But I wouldn't trade that for anything else.

ALAN SIPPY

I said 'Araam se', Sachin replied 'Bindaas'

It must have been God's will, or else why would I be at the other end when Sachin Tendulkar scored a hundred on his Ranji Trophy debut. I scored a hundred in the same innings, but I remember the little boy's knock more than mine. I was privileged to be at the non-striker's end as it was my claim to fame.

It was late in 1988, and the Mumbai team didn't have the then India captain Dilip Vengsarkar, vice-captain Ravi Shastri, and Chandrakant Pandit as they were playing a series against New Zealand. By then, I had played a few seasons for Mumbai. There were established names like Shishir Hattangadi, skipper Lalchand Rajput, Raju Kulkarni, and Sudarshan Kulkarni, to name a few, during our camp.

Sachin had already become a name due to his exploits in school cricket, but when we were told he had been picked for the Mumbai team, some of us tempered our expectations as first class is a different level. So, a few days before that Gujarat game (December 10–12, 1988), Sachin Tendulkar walked to attend the Mumbai nets.

An innocent, shy little kid. Myself, Shishir and Lalu (Rajput) were like big daddies in the absence of stars. We were apprehensive that he doesn't get injured. However, Raju Kulkarni and other pacers went easy on the nets on the first day, and he didn't look slightly unsettled. I thought the kid was showing bravado and trying to fit in a man's world.

I went home that day, and my dad asked who's this new kid as he was reading about him in the papers. 'Nothing special, but I hope the kid doesn't get hurt, Dad.'

As fate would have it, when we batted second after Gujarat, Lalu (Rajput) had a decent partnership and were well set going into lunch. I am trying to remember who the manager was as we didn't have coaches in those days; Ramakant Desai told us he was planning to send Sachin at No. 4. 'Whoever stays at the wicket, please take care and guide the kid.'

It was December humidity in Mumbai; we were both sitting with towels wrapped around and, just for the heck of it, said, 'Yeah, yeah, it's alright.' The truth is that we didn't even bother. When Lalu got out, it was Sachin who walked in. So, when he walked past me, I just looked at him and said, 'Araam se,' and the one-word reply came, 'Bindaas.'

I was impressed by his confidence.

The Gujarat close-in fielders were sledging him both

in Hindi and Gujarati. I thought it must be baptism by fire for him, but a couple of ferocious cover drives later, I turned back towards Wankhede's dressing room, looked at our manager, and playfully gestured, 'You wanted me to take care of this fellow. Does he even remotely need my guidance?'

He would give a sheepish green between overs, and his body language suggested, 'Just chill, Alan, I have got this one.' I wasn't panicking, but I wanted to know if someone could be so talented at just 15 and a half years.

I scored 127, and Sachin scored a brilliant century. It doesn't happen often, but I was very depressed as I went home that evening. Let me just clarify that my depression stemmed more out of fear of how my father was going to hammer me verbally. My dad didn't even bother congratulating me for my hundred, as it wasn't a bad knock either.

He pounced on me, 'Alan, you told me he was just another kid.' I just could gibberish-ly murmur, 'I am so sorry, Dad. I didn't have an idea that this kid is so special. He is from a different planet. He is different.' I told my father that players like us could keep playing for the next 100 years, but this was a different level of genius.

I did play another couple of years for Mumbai and a few more games here and there, but I also played with him for CCI in local tourneys. I can tell you one thing from those days of the late 80s and early 90s. As one could see that Bombay was all set to produce its next global cricket superstar, and everyone around him wanted to appropriate Sachin.

You don't become a hanger if you are intelligent enough, so the relationship is cordial. To this day, we share a good relationship. You can become a superstar overnight, but to hold on to your stardom for 35 years with so much humility makes him unique.

Even today, if we bump into each other at a party, and he speaks for two to three minutes, he will listen to you with rapt attention. So that's his way of being endearing and respectful at the same time. He would make you feel that only you matter in those two to three minutes.

I am not Sachin's story. Sachin is my story.

RAJU KULKARNI

Ferrari ki Sawari at 4 in the morning

It was a function organized by the Maharashtra Cricket Association on the sidelines of the Ranji match between Mumbai and Maharashtra during the late 80s. Unfortunately, age is catching up with me, so don't ask me for the date. It was an evening function, and a full-strength Mumbai team was in attendance. The two stalwarts Dilip Vengsarkar, who had already played 100 Tests and Ravi Shastri, with 70-match experience, along with Chandrakant Pandit and myself, both having already played for India, were present there.

It was before Sachin made his Ranji Trophy debut, but he was travelling with the team as he was already known as the next big thing. I will explain why that evening in Pune is still fresh in my memory. If you have four Mumbai cricketers sitting together, the discussions will be serious cricketing ones undoubtedly. And who was being discussed by the four Test players? A 15-year-old rookie yet to make his first-class debut whom we have only seen in Mumbai nets.

'I think Sachin will play 100 Tests,' said Dilip, the second Indian man after Sunny (Gavaskar) to complete that landmark that was so rare back in the 80s. Ravi stopped Dilip and said: 'I think he will play no less than 150 Test matches if he keeps this work ethic and the talent he has got. Nobody can stop him.' Chandu and I were stunned as this was being discussed by the two stars of Indian cricket about a boy who has only shown his talent, and the real Test was yet to begin.

This story needed to be told to give you an idea of what kind of assessment the hard-core Mumbaikars did of Sachin's talent. Since he arrived as a child prodigy after his world record in school cricket, failure has never been an option for Sachin. He was destined to succeed, and he did. So no one is surprised if they have seen him from close quarters since he stepped into the Mumbai Ranji nets.

I remember bowling to him on that first day in the 1988 season, and he wasn't wearing a helmet. Many people didn't wear helmets compulsorily, even in the late 80s. When he first took stance, I didn't go full throttle at him, but once I saw him play everything comfortably, I started bowling full pace.

For me, a cherished moment was an inter probables match with the Mumbai team at the Wankhede back in 1988, where I had Sachin dismissed. He was caught and bowled; that was the only time I got his wicket. I remember in Aurangabad that year, Sachin wasn't picked in the main squad, and with all players available, he wasn't getting a fair share of batting at nets.

I had an extended net session, and I saw him stand quietly on one side. I told him to pad up. As I started bowling, he said in Marathi, which in Hindi would be: 'Thoda pace se daal na'. It was so endearing that I couldn't help but laugh.

I often told Sachin that if cricket as a subject had been taught at IIT, IIM or Harvard, he would be the most qualified professor of the subject. A match that I can remember is our 1-run defeat to Haryana in the 1991 Ranji Trophy final.

Sachin missed a hundred, but that six off Kapil Dev was special. Haryana had a better chance of winning, but Dilip and Sachin brought us back into the match. After that next year, I was the Mumbai skipper, but Sachin was away on national duty. But we always had a great relationship off the field. Although I was much older than him, we shared a good rapport.

In fact, professionally, I worked with Sachin on a project in 1999, and for that, we had to meet multiple times in England that summer, where I had also gone for my business-related work. But on a personal note, my evergreen Tendulkar anecdote would be being one of the first to ride his gleaming red Ferrari.

Sachin is crazy about cars, and that's a well-documented fact, but that evening I got a call from him. 'Raju, my Ferrari will be delivered today from Australia around midnight. I will come to your place around 4 am, and we will go on a spin. Tell your son, too,' he said.

My son Varun was a teenager then, and he was instantly excited that Sachin Tendulkar would come to pick us up. His eyes were on the clock; after that, Sachin didn't call. Finally, I told my son I didn't think he would come. 'He will accept the delivery at that hour in the night. He would be tired and would certainly go home. So he isn't coming today,' I told my son.

I had fallen asleep when the doorbell rang at precisely 4 am. Sachin was standing and asking us to join him on a ride. Frankly speaking, I found the seat beside the driver uncomfortable, but I somehow managed.

Now the side view mirror of the Ferrari is huge, and I wondered how one can drive through maddening Mumbai traffic with that kind of a part. I asked Sachin if this mirror gets damaged on the road or if there is a glitch in any part? Unfortunately, there isn't any Ferrari service centre in India. He laughed and said: 'For any damage or glitch, I will have to call the Singapore centre of Ferrari, and they will send their engineers to check.'

I could only mumble, 'Thank You very much.'

The Ferrari Ki Sawaari on that nippy Mumbai night enjoying the beauty of Maximum City with a world-beater would remain one helluva experience.

VIGNESH SHAHANE

I have known Sachin at many levels. First, I played with him and against him while growing up in Mumbai and while aspiring to play for the state and the country. Second, we became friends over a period of time, and finally, Sachin is the brand ambassador of the company I work for as Chief Executive Officer. So it has been a relationship that goes back nearly 40 years.

The first time I heard of Sachin was when he was 10–11. In fact, that was the first time I had seen him. It was before his exploits for Shardashram with Vinod Kambli and before he had set the school cricket scene on fire. We were playing a B-division Kanga league game and the wicket was a minefield. Batting was near impossible, and we were all out for 65 against Sassanians, the club for which Sachin had turned up. However, the wicket was such that 65 was

Vignesh is the CEO of Ageas Federal Life Insurance Company which has Sachin as their brand ambassador.

considered competitive, and we had a decent chance of making a match of it. And in fact, we had reduced Sassanians to 30/5 when Sachin walked in. He carried an oversized bat and wasn't much taller than the wicket. Scrawny and small, we felt we could have this little boy for breakfast. We were mistaken, and Sachin scored 28 or so and carried his team to victory. At the end of the game, our entire team got together and discussed this tiny little boy. Each of us was in awe and agreed that someone extraordinary had arrived on the scene.

We have all been proved right. Within months Sachin had taken over the school cricket scene, and his exploits as a batsman were being spoken about by everyone in Mumbai. At times it was impossible to get him out. A few years later, when we travelled to play an age group tournament for Mumbai, we realised how good he was. Sachin scored a double hundred in each of the games and got out stumped to a spinner after his double ton and after he had set up the win for us. He got out just because he was bored. No one could actually get him out.

After that, we would meet off and on and became friends. We would meet at parties and social events, and I never thought we would work closely together soon enough. At the time, I was still trying to find my way through age-group cricket while Sachin was already an Indian cricketer and doing things the world had never seen.

My next real engagement with Sachin happened when I

took over as Chief Executive of IDBI Federal Life Insurance Company. We were ranked number 17 in the country in the pecking order and were looking to climb up the ladder and transform ourselves. That's when someone suggested we look at Sachin Tendulkar as a brand ambassador. First, we all thought this wasn't going to work. Yes, Sachin had retired, but he was still cricket's No. 1 brand, and here we were at number 17. But then we decided to go ahead and, in eight months, had made it to the top 10. Sachin, believe it or not, had made this possible. He had instilled self-belief among all our colleagues within months of becoming our brand ambassador. There was a spring in people's stride, and they would all come into office with renewed purpose. The understanding was if Sachin Tendulkar was batting for us, we, too, needed to step up and couldn't continue to play like a lowly-ranked team. We needed to justify to Sachin that we deserved to have him as our brand ambassador.

We, as a company, decided to invest in marathons and, within years, had been able to reach out to a lac of people around the country who would all take part largely to see Sachin. He was the glue in the four cities we had our marathons. He was the pied piper who made these events a huge success, and we could reach out to the masses in no time.

The best thing about Sachin as a brand ambassador is his punctuality and discipline. For marathons, we often had a call time of 3:30 am in the morning and never has Sachin been a minute late. In fact, one time in Kolkata, a friend of mine wanted to meet him, and I asked him to come at 3 am in the morning. That was the only available time, and I was sure he wouldn't take me up on the offer and wouldn't turn up at that ungodly hour. But, to my surprise, he did. It was Sachin, after all; maybe I had underestimated what he meant to all of us in India. My friend had come at 2.58 am and asked if Sachin was around. I remember telling him that wait for two minutes, and he will soon see Sachin. Believe it or not, precisely two minutes later, the door to the elevator opened, and Sachin stepped out. I looked at my friend, and he was utterly stunned. That's what makes Sachin so unique.

Now as the CEO of Ageas Federal, let me share something very personal. And I haven't said this to anyone. Not even Sachin. When he played for India at number 4 and batted, there was a sense of calm in the country. With Sachin out there, we knew things couldn't go wrong. He was there for us all was the common Indian sentiment. As the brand ambassador of Ageas Federal, Sachin is batting at number 4 for the brand. And with him out there batting for us, nothing can ever go wrong for Ageas Federal Life Insurance. He is our best protective shield, and I couldn't have asked for anyone better than him as my brand ambassador. It has been a privilege knowing him and working closely together. Happy birthday Sachin.

SANJEEV SHARMA

I was playing against Sachin Tendulkar on his Irani Cup debut in 1989.

I remember Dilip Vengsarkar talking to Kapil Dev about Sachin and insisting on how great a prospect he is. Be it Kapil or anyone else, the general notion was that he was too young and had a long way to go because he had only played school cricket then. For most of us, he was another kid with a bundle of talent. They all thought he was outstanding but needed more exposure. Very few could gauge what stature he could gain. We never could have imagined he would scale the heights he has done. He set standards altogether.

People talk about how he showed glimpses of his genius by tearing into Abdul Qadir during an exhibition match in Pakistan during his first tour to Pakistan in late 1989, but people started taking him more seriously during an

Sanjeev Sharma (former India pacer) gives a dressing room account of the journey from Irani debut to his first Test century.

Australia-Asia Cup match in Sharjah in April 1990. Before the game began, the Pakistani squad members told us in crude Punjabi: 'We have made a special plan for your little batsman.' We wondered what it could be. But when Sachin walked out to bat on a typically docile Sharjah pitch, we got a whiff of the plan. Wasim Akram deliberately overstepped by a long way to bowl a bouncer so that he could hurry Sachin. The bouncer hit his helmet and went for a boundary. We knew they were trying to rattle the kid. Next ball, Akram pitched it full, probably expecting Sachin to be on his backfoot. But Sachin confidently plonked his front foot forward and hammered it to the cover boundary. We closely followed Imran Khan's gesture. He pointed to Akram from cover, saying be careful with this boy; he is special. Sachin then had a fascination for walkmans (portable music players), and he finally got his yellow walkman in Sharjah on that tour.

Sachin grew in stature with his maiden Test century, which helped India save the match at Manchester in the summer of 1990. I was there in the dressing room. He was hitting the ball at will. He defied the norm of waiting for the bad ball. Batsmen, these days, demolish good deliveries thanks to T20 cricket. But Sachin could do it back then as well. His punch was extraordinary against the likes of Angus Fraser, Chris Lewis and Devon Malcolm. For an Indian to dominate in those conditions was very rare. The entire English team gave him a standing ovation. I remember

Graham Gooch rushing to our dressing room and telling us, 'You have an exceptional player. He is made for greater things.'

After his first tour to England, he decided to play county cricket. That's why he was back in England the following year, playing for Yorkshire, which plays its cricket in the most challenging conditions. That spoke for his will to learn.

Sanjeev spoke to Arani Basu in 2013,
just before Tendulkar's farewell Test

AAKASH CHOPRA

Sachin, the person, is the tallest of 'em all

My first interaction with Sachin happened in Ahmedabad when I was named in the Indian team for the first time for a series against New Zealand in October 2003. Like everyone else, I also looked up to him as that idol, a maestro that you always thought was the pinnacle and exactly where you aspired to be if you could go that far.

I realised early that Sachin goes to great lengths to make you feel comfortable and part of the group. Because he always knew that all these kids idolised him, and he was very humble about it. He quietly does his bit to welcome you with open arms.

There were separate bowlers and batters meeting before that Test match against New Zealand. He would ask me six or seven questions during the batters' meeting. For e.g., 'Has Dan Vettori bowled an arm ball? Whether Daryl Tuffey is bowling the leg cutter?' The questions were about the warm-up games I played against New Zealand.

I used to wonder, I might have played a few deliveries from these bowlers but Sachin has faced hundreds of those kinds of deliveries, and how can I be of any help? So it was his way of breaking the ice, and very sweet of him to do so with newcomers.

Anyone who walks into that dressing room, your eyes would be transfixed on the floor, and if Sachin Tendulkar is around, you won't even open your mouth. So he was always cognizant that kids walking in the dressing room would be in awe of Sachin Tendulkar, the player. So, Sachin Tendulkar, the man, always did his bit to make you feel part of the setup.

During my time in the national team, he would ask, 'Aakash, would you mind standing behind the stumps?' Of course, I would have stood there anyway, as there is so much to learn. What better place to stand and learn batting? 'Just peeche khade ho jaao aur unko (Tendulkar) khelte huye dekho.'

The way he reacts to every ball is the coaching manual right in front of you. So I would stand there always. In fact, he would ask questions if his footwork was correct or if the shuffle, he was trying was coming out well? Watching the ball close enough? I would be embarrassed that why is Paaji asking me? But he would continue to ask.

I remember I got a chance to interact with him in Ahmedabad because I wasn't sure how many Test matches, I would play. So, I sought his permission and went to his room. He gave me an hour, and I had plenty of questions. He, in fact, told me that he was not able to sleep properly for 15 days prior, and he was visualising every ball. How would he play Wasim, Waqar and Shoaib? That initial awkwardness that we newcomers had evaporated quickly.

We ended up chatting about cricket, and when he came for commentary in the 2019 World Cup, he once again asked me, 'Kya soch raha, pitch kaisa hone wallah hai?' Just chatting along and talking cricket. Sachin has been that person who has inspired us all. Sachin Tendulkar, the player, stood out initially, but what stands out for me now is Sachin Tendulkar, the person.

He is phenomenal.

You reach out to him, and I know if you reach out to him, he will do everything he can to help you.

We all love you, Paaji.

SURESH RAINA

Sachin Paaji is special. Always will be. The greatest batsman to have played the game. But that's not what defines him. He is a wonderful human being, and that's what I will always say is his first quality. I fondly remember Sachin Paaji taking me out to dinner when I got my first Test century in Colombo. He had scored a double hundred in the same game and had taken me out to my first Japanese meal. It was an experience. Paaji was a foodie, and with him around, we learnt a lot about Japanese food. He came up to me in the evening and said it was time to celebrate my century, and he would take us, Yuvi, Bhajju pa and me, out to dinner. That's what Sachin Paaji is all about. He was the perfect team man who always celebrated our success as his own.

However, my most memorable Sachin Paaji story has to be the 2011 World Cup. I was 25 at the time and not in the team for the initial few games. In fact, I was doing everything I could to attract attention, that I was the best option at number six. I would spend maximum time doing fielding practice and was determined to make a case to Gary and Mahi bhai for my inclusion. Playing the World Cup at home was a dream, and playing Australia and Pakistan were two of the biggest occasions for any player playing the sport.

And then, in the quarter-final against Australia, I was sitting next to Paaji in the dressing room when he said, 'Look at this as an opportunity. A World Cup quarter-final with 78 runs left, and you have a chance to win it for the country. It is your day; go win it for India.'

India was 187/5, and it was my turn to make a difference. I have been a Tendulkar fan since childhood and was lost for a second or two. It was Sachin Paaji who was speaking to me. He had waited for six World Cups to win the trophy. And here he was urging me to do it for him and India. With Dhoni out and 75 runs still to get, I could not have asked for a better opportunity to make a mark. All I told him was, 'Paaji aaj jita ke aayeenge [Will win it for India tonight, elder brother]'.

I made a 28-ball 34 and was unbeaten that night. Of course, these weren't many runs considering the asking rate towards the close of the innings. But that near-one-hour stint batting with Yuvraj was perhaps the most invigorating one hour for each of us.

All Yuvi Paaji and I saw was Brett Lee, Mitchell Johnson and the others. To tell you the truth, even when I hit those boundaries or sixes, I did not feel any sense of elation. The job still needed to be finished. All I was thinking was I had got this opportunity after a lot of effort and couldn't let it go. I had to do it for Sachin Paaji. And for my country.

Right through the tournament, we used to listen to Sachin Paaji. There was something about him this tournament. First, he played some great cricket himself; he had scored two hundreds already. And when he said our fans wanted us to win, you could see a very different type of confidence in his eyes. He was calm but confident, and we drew inspiration from him.

Most recently, I played with and under Paaji in the Road Safety series. Firstly it is an important cause, and we were determined to create awareness, for there are far too many accidents. Second, we were playing as India, and that's what matters to each one of us. Third, we were wearing the India logo, and when you do that, things are very different. Sachin Paaji, as captain, played the tournament with the same seriousness that he did as a player. At the start of the tournament, he addressed us in the dressing room and emphasised that we were all there to win it for India. He meant business. He would set an example during training, and you could see his seriousness. On the field, he has always been an astute leader. He is involved and reads the game exceptionally well. These are hallmarks of a good captain, and it was a matter of great satisfaction to have won the tournament twice in a row under his leadership.

As Sachin Paaji turns 50, may he keep inspiring us. Spending each moment with him in the changing room is an experience, and I want to have many more years of Sachin Paaji guiding and teaching us all.

JATIN PARANJAPE

That Sachin was meant to be the best in the world was very apparent from the day I saw him bat for the first time. In fact, he was brought into this world to play cricket. His love for the game only matched and surpassed his audacious talent.

In his early years, he was looked after by Achrekar sir, like his son. Achrekar sir would take him on his two-wheeler to multiple matches on the same day, and this honed his match play tremendously. It also had a significant role in his ability to express himself at the crease as he played in so many practice games as an 11- or 12-year-old. This extensive match plays completely peeled away the slight intimidation that one feels while playing a match as opposed to just having a net.

Another excellent step for Sachin was playing for the Cricket Club of India, which allowed him to be around some of the past greats of Indian cricket. Add to that a great pitch to bat on, and Sachin was soon on his way. The Irani Trophy hundred saw him rightly being picked for the Pakistan tour, and History was just starting to be written.

I will never forget a story that Ravi Shastri once told me about that Pakistan tour—I think it was the first test match, and Sachin had just got out. He came and sat next to Ravi and did not say anything for the first few minutes. But then he asked Ravi, 'Ghaee keli na (I was too much in a hurry, wasn't I?)? That story astounded me—such a lot of self-confidence from that early stage, wherein he knew that he had a grasp of international cricket! It remains one of my favourite stories.

I used to try and call him after every century early on in his career. I remember speaking to him after the Perth hundred, and he said that not only the wicket but the outfield has tremendous bounce too! He has a whacky sense of humour and is one of the best one-liner specialists I have known.

I was with him for the game after his father passed away, and he barely said a word. He was very sad but knew he had to get back and play as soon as possible. Cricket was always a priority.

Sachin was also a lovely teammate. He was very positive, and he loved his teammates succeeding! He would often tell me if I had got out early, 'Don't worry, Jats, next innings hai na or Don't worry, Jats, the ball was there for that shot, and you went for it'. He was a player's captain and, I might add, very unfairly underrated as a captain by our friends from the media. I enjoyed playing under him for Mumbai; we had a blast! If we finished a match early, we would go out into the nets again for a couple of hours, and then a big feast of biryani would follow that Sachin would have already organized.

A lot of cricketing nous has been passed on by Sachin to every cricketer in the Mumbai and Indian teams. These pieces of knowledge and experience transfer have had a big hand in the successes of individual players and the Indian team as a whole over the last few years. Sachin's room used to be a melting pot after an Indian team game where the match was broken down and minutely dissected with some pearls of wisdom shared by Sachin.

I have been fortunate to see him from a young age and have been his friend since we were 10–11. Would want to wish him all the very best for the future on his 50th birthday.

M.S.K. PRASAD

**Of treating teammates as equals and turning
V.V.S. Laxman's career around**

I met Sachin Tendulkar for the first time during the 1998
Commonwealth Games in Kuala Lumpur. Cricket was a part
of that Games. That was the first time I played with Sachin.
I had made my India debut a few months earlier. I used to
look up to him already, even though he was precisely two
years older. We even share our birthdays.

During that CWG, I was constantly watching him. I used
to follow how he spoke, his walk, or anything he did. I kept
on looking at him. Sachin noticed it. He felt a little strange.
'What is it that this bugger is always looking at and making
me uncomfortable?' he would think.

In one of the team meetings, I was just staring at him.
Rohan Gavaskar was also a part of the team. He called
Rohan and asked what my problem was. After that, Rohan
was tasked to ask me why I was doing it.

Then Rohan came and asked me, 'Macha, Sachin said that you are constantly staring at him. Why are you behaving like that?'

'I can't believe I am playing alongside the person I adored all through. Coming from smaller states like Andhra, it is such a big thing to play with a person of this stature. I understand playing for India is the biggest thing, but playing alongside him was even bigger,' I replied.

Rohan went and informed Sachin that I was overawed by his presence. That same evening, Sachin came to me and started talking. He took me out for a walk. While walking, he said: 'All these things (adulation, fame and popularity) are there till we are playing for the country. When we are representing the country, Sachin Tendulkar and M.S.K. Prasad are equals. Don't ever feel you are inferior to me or somebody else is superior. All 15 members of the Indian team are equals.'

Whatever gap I felt, he built the bridge for me in a few minutes.

He is one person who always likes to spend time with youngsters. You will rarely see him sitting separately with senior cricketers. Instead, he always shared his best moments with younger players. That's how Ajit Agarkar and Harbhajan Singh became so close to him.

Many people judged Sachin's captaincy with that tough tour of Australia in 1999–2000. However, people don't realise that only Sachin and Javagal Srinath had prior playing experience in Australia. Sourav Ganguly went to Australia in 1992 but hardly played a game. Everyone else, including Rahul Dravid and V.V.S. Laxman, was travelling to Australia for the first time.

We had played 40 days of home matches before travelling. Once our series with New Zealand was over, we were on the plane to Australia in three days. By the time the players could acclimatise, the tour was over. When Sachin took over the captaincy, Indian cricket underwent a major transition. People only talk in numbers, but only a few look at who built a system.

I would like to narrate one story here to elaborate on Sachin's man-management skills. After we lost the first Test match in Adelaide, Sachin, V.V.S. Laxman, and I went for a walk and a meal. We were discussing how we need to adjust in the remaining matches. Then the conversation veered towards who were our favourite players. I said I liked Dravid, Ganguly and Laxman. Laxman also took a couple of names.

Then Laxman asked Sachin about his favourite player. Sachin replied: 'Laxman if you don't smile and show your teeth, I'll say you are my favourite player.'

Laxman started laughing and said Sachin was only making fun of him. Sachin interrupted and added: 'Laxman, I'll tell you one thing. You are blessed with so much talent. You can see the ball a split second earlier than me. God has given you exceptional talent which you are not able to understand. God gave me minimum talent, which I am maximising. I have four gears in my batting—defence, push, drive and loft. I understand the conditions and use my logic and perform accordingly.

'You have so much talent that you can straightaway bat on fourth gear. You see the ball so early that you don't worry about the conditions. That way, sometimes you click, and sometimes you fail. The day you realise the value of the first three gears, you will become a legend of the game.'

After that conversation, I saw a different V.V.S. Laxman. We opened together later in the tour, and he got 167 in the Sydney Test match. After that, there has been no looking back for Laxman.

As a captain, he never put any sort of pressure on us during that tour. He knew we were all youngsters. Sachin never demanded anything from his players. He wanted to lead by example. He worked so hard on his game. On that tour, he was given a suite room. He removed all the sofas in the room and asked Ajit Agarkar to bowl fast at him with wet balls. He was so engrossed in his game. Sachin doesn't need to talk. His mere presence is a learning for youngsters.

JOYDEEP MUKHERJEE

I am not here to comment on how good Sachin Tendulkar was as a player. He was the greatest. Period. I would instead share two stories that will help us understand Sachin better. Each time Sachin came to Kolkata we would make it a point to go to the Kali temple together. One time it was on a Sunday afternoon when the roads were half empty, with most taking their leisurely siesta. We were in South Kolkata on Hazra, a kilometre from the Kalighat Kali Temple. Accompanying us was Harbhajan Singh, who was in the back seat of the car while I was driving with Sachin sitting next to me. Bhajji had his glass rolled down, and a few young men on a motorbike recognised him. You know what it is like with Indian cricketers. When some started shouting Bhajji Bhajji and following us, Harbhajan quietly looked out the window and said, 'Mera naam kyun kehe rehe ho Boss to samne baithe huwe hain.'

This was enough. By the time we reached Kalighat, a cavalcade of motorbikes was following us. And when we came out after the darshan, I had more than a few people on the car's bonnet and about 500 crowding my vehicle. I was very concerned for my car because I knew Sachin and Bhajji would go away while my car would have permanent dents! It was only after Sachin came out and waved to the fans that they let us go and my car was saved.

The second story was when Sachin had come to Kolkata in 1994 to play for East Bengal in the P. Sen Trophy final against Mohun Bagan. We had lost a couple of finals to Mohun Bagan and had brought in the best of India, including Sachin and Kapil Dev, for the final. Sachin, 21, was captaining us, and it was an experience to see him up close and follow his routine. Suddenly he got out his eau de toilette from his black kit bag and started spraying it liberally on his helmet, pads and more. I had not seen anyone do this and asked him why he was doing so. He said he wanted to smell good when he was out there, and these things were a part of him. And may I say he just said it with a degree of simplicity you won't see in many. Smell good! How good was that!

He is an extraordinary man, and all of India loved to go to bed knowing Sachin would bat the next day. This habit lasted 24 years—a habit we all loved. Wish you a happy 50th birthday Sachin.

KIRAN MORE

Of throwing and bowling competitions with
Kapil Dev and helping India dominate Pakistan

I met Sachin Tendulkar for the first time in Baroda during a Ranji Trophy match. He was picked for Bombay (now Mumbai) when he was barely 15. That was his first tour outside Bombay. Chandrakant Pandit was a very dear friend of mine. I had invited him for lunch at my house. Chandrakant asked me if he could bring Sachin with him. Sachin came to my house and had a quiet dinner, but he was most excited about a blue Maruti car I had.

Next, I saw him when the Indian team practised before the West Indies tour in 1989. Sachin was called to the nets. He had already become the talk of the town. And then, he was picked for the famous Pakistan tour later that year. That's when he showed the world what he could become.

We had a very young team for that Pakistan tour. Sanjay Manjrekar was also very young. Then there were Salil Ankola and Vivek Razdan in the team. But people in Pakistan were only talking about Sachin. The local people were eager to see Sachin. The first glimpse of his talent and resilience was during the Test match in Sialkot. The pitch was green and aided seam bowling. Pakistan had an out-and-out pace attack. They wanted to hurt us with pace rather than looking for wickets first. Sachin got hit in the nose. But he showed no pain, and his brave half-century helped us draw the match.

But Sachin became a sensation during the unofficial match in Peshawar. There was rain and very little chance of the game being played. So Ravi Shastri and I went to the market to buy Peshawar's famous 'jootis'. By the time we reached the stadium, the crowd was making noise. Sachin was batting against the legend of leg spin Abdul Qadir. Sachin went after Qadir and smashed him for four sixes. Qadir was called Bauji by his teammates. We heard the Pakistan players wear teasing their Bauji for getting hit all around the park by a 16-year-old.

The way Sachin played on that tour gave confidence to Indian batters that we could dominate Pakistan bowlers. After that, we started beating Pakistan a lot more in Sharjah. He played Wasim Akram the best.

Pakistani players used to call him Giddu because of his height. I once overheard Imran Khan telling his teammates in Sharjah: '*Bas Giddu ko out kar lo jaldi. Baki ko hum dekh lenge* (Just get Giddu out quickly. Then, we will take care of the rest.).' That's the kind of impact Sachin had.

We could make out how confident he was about his skills. That Indian dressing room on that tour has to be the noisiest one I have been part of. He shared a bond with Kapil Dev straight away. He and Kapil Paaji would have throwing competitions. They used to stand at the centre of stadiums and throw past the boundary. Sachin used to imitate the bowling actions of established bowlers like Imran Khan and Malcolm Marshall. Salil and Sachin used to do that all the time.

We were put up at a guest house owned by a football manufacturer. Sachin's brother Ajeet was allowed to stay with him since he was young. He had the habit of sleepwalking. We were not allowed to go out on the streets much. But Sachin turned that guest house into a happening place. He played badminton and table tennis with everyone. But Kapil Paaji was always there with him.

After that, we travelled to New Zealand. There, I had a partnership with him, and he narrowly missed out on a hundred. He cried a lot. He had the passion and desperately wanted that first hundred. I felt so bad for him.

Sachin may have been soft-spoken. But he was very aggressive with the bat. He wanted to dominate bowlers all the time. We used to call him Viv Richards of Indian cricket.

That first Test hundred finally came in Manchester in 1990. That was a memorable innings. The shots he played on the up were astonishing. Everyone used to discuss that those aggressive shots would get him into trouble. But he pulled them off with that heavy bat of his. Bishan Bedi was the coach of the Indian team. I was slated to go in to bat next when he was batting with Manoj Prabhakar. We all wanted Sachin to get that hundred. I was moving around the dressing room, juggling balls. Bedi sir told me to sit quietly at one place till Sachin got his hundred.

Then we went to Australia in 1991–92. That tour gives me goosebumps. Sachin's hundred at WACA in Perth has to be in the top 5 while rating all his hundreds. That pitch was something different. Mike Whitney's ball to Navjyot Sidhu hit a crack and flew to the second slip. It was so hard to bat.

Again, I had the best seat to watch that masterclass. Sachin and I were room partners. He used to shut down when he got into match mode. Sachin and I shared an 80-run partnership in that Test match. The shots he played off the backfoot were incredible. To cut and drive in front of the wicket on a pitch with such pace and bounce was incredible. I could see Dean Jones and Allan Border looking at each other and saying 'wow' when Sachin was on strike. Aussies play a very aggressive brand of cricket, and their appreciation of Sachin was also not subtle.

Sachin's bowling was also evolving on that tour, followed by the World Cup. He had a beautiful release and strong shoulders. He could bowl outswing and inswing. Then he would bowl his leg breaks and googlies. Sachin always stayed active during practice sessions. Once he was done batting, he would bowl in the nets. And he got into competition with Kapil Paaji in the nets. He would challenge Kapil Paaji to outswing or inswing competitions. He bowled so well on that tour that he also became an essential bowler for us in the World Cup.

Everyone remembers Javed Miandad's spot jumps while reacting to me in that 1992 World Cup match. But it was during Sachin's over that he was really tied down. He was getting frustrated. Sachin bowled 10 overs in that game after he set the game up with a brilliant unbeaten half-century. We were feeling a lot of pressure going into that match. It was the first time India and Pakistan played in a World Cup. Sachin rose to the occasion. Sachin helped India start its dominance over Pakistan in World Cups.

ROHIT SHARMA

It was ahead of the tour game against Australia in 2004–05, and I was practising at the nets of the Cricket Club of India. That's when I had my first close encounter with Paaji. The first of many. Paaji had come to the CCI and was standing behind our nets and was watching me train. I have to confess I was nervous. It was natural I would be. Here was someone who was instrumental in me starting to play cricket. In our household, cricket meant Sachin Tendulkar. The TV would be switched on and off depending on how Sachin Tendulkar batted. And when you have the same person standing behind you and watching you play, it's a surreal feeling. You just wanted to impress him. To get recognition in his eyes was the ultimate yardstick. Thereafter we played the 2006 Ranji Trophy final together, which Mumbai won, and I kept learning from seeing Paaji up close. Frankly, all you needed to do was observe. Follow up closely and see how he went about his drills. What he would do at the nets, for he was always the epitome of perfection. And that's what

I was trying to imbibe. Whatever little I could learn would do me good in my career.

Our first real partnership happened in the final of the CB series in Australia. We needed a partnership to win the contest, and Paaji was batting brilliantly. It was important I stayed with him and backed him up. The final was being played in the aftermath of an intense Test series, and much was at stake. Australia had claimed that they would close out the three match final in just two games, and we needed to turn up at our best. We did and beat them 2–0. The third final was not required, and Paaji was brilliant in the two finals. He was reading the bowlers exceptionally well and could understand what they were about to bowl to me. In fact, he would come up and tell me what to expect, and it was of great help. I could trust his judgment while batting, which helped me make an important contribution to the team. Ultimately, it turned out to be a match-winning partnership and was a hugely satisfying moment for Paaji, me, and the entire team.

To be honest, I have a lot of stories with Paaji and memories that are countless. If I start to recall all of them, I will consume reams of newsprint. So instead, let me just say a couple of things. Growing up in Mumbai, Sachin Tendulkar was second to God for me. He was a part of my growing up. My inspiration to play the sport has made me what I am. Cricket in our household meant Sachin Tendulkar. He was the yardstick in everything that we did. If you wanted to be the best, you needed to try and bat like Sachin Tendulkar. He was the defacto coaching manual. And then, to be able to play with him meant the world to me. It was like I was living my dream to share the same dressing room, discuss batting with him, and make plans together. We played years together for the Mumbai Indians, and Paaji was hugely supportive of me each time. Finally, in 2013 I even got to captain the man I considered my idol. Think about it for a second. He was my role model, and now I was captaining him in the IPL. These are things you dream about. In my case, dreams have come true. When I became the captain of MI, Paaji was always there for me as a sounding board. I could go up to him and discuss plans and draw on his experience. To have someone with his level of cricketing genius on the field was a huge plus for us in Mumbai.

I also want to talk about getting my Test cap from Paaji. The West Indies versus India series in November 2013, was all about Sachin Tendulkar. He was playing his 199th and 200th Test, and emotion was outpouring everywhere. With Paaji having announced that this was his last series, the sentiment was very different. Each of us was emotional and wanted to make him feel special every second he was with us. In fact, for us in the team, we had to do something special for him and ensure we won the series. It was deeply satisfying to be able to score a 100 and contribute to the team's effort after we had been reduced to 83/5 at Eden Gardens. Paaji was very pleased, and so was I. To make my

Test debut in his 199th Test and then make a contribution will always be a very special memory. I was able to score another hundred in his last Test match at the Wankhede, and it was fantastic to see Paaji score a very good 74. It was evidence of how focused he was even on his 200th Test.

For us who play international cricket scoring a hundred is a yardstick. It is one of the most difficult things to do. It is about concentration and commitment. And when you score 100 international hundreds over 24 years, you must be someone of a different level. Paaji was, and I was fortunate to be able to play with him and even captain him in the IPL.

As I said at the start of this piece, Sachin Tendulkar was my role model and inspiration. He was the benchmark. Still is and always will be. As Paaji turns 50, I want to wish him a very happy birthday and good health in the coming months and years. He has enriched our sport as a true devotee, and it is fair to say that there will never be another Sachin Tendulkar. Happy 50th birthday, Paaji.

Quotes from other teammates

I've played alongside him for so long. Sachin played under different captains. I think in 2000 he decided that he is not going to captain anymore when he was such a senior player, such a legend of the game. But to adjust and contribute to the progress of Indian cricket under different captains, and to help them flourish as captains, is something only a role model and inspiration like Sachin can do—which he did really good. The legacy that he left behind is not only scoring hundreds, double hundreds and 100 hundreds, but also the way he inspired the younger generation of Indian cricketers and the world cricketers. I still remember Kane Williamson in his debut Test match in Ahmedabad; chatting with Sachin, understanding the game.

—V.V.S. Laxman on *Star Sports*

When we first met. I felt I have shaken hands with God. You have guided me in my toughest phases. You taught me to believe in my abilities. I'll play the same role for youngsters that you played for me.

—Yuvraj Singh on Twitter

He's changed the landscape, both on and off the field, for Indian cricket over the last two decades. It's almost mindboggling. A whole generation has grown up with Tendulkar. They've seen his ups and downs and lived their lives and dreams through his feats. So many people in India want to be a cricketer. A legend. The greatest player that I've played with as a batsman. He's been a huge inspiration. To see a 16-year-old boy do what he did was unbelievable. It defied imagination and was a huge inspiration for me. I felt like if he could do it then I should also try to be a Test cricketer.

—Rahul Dravid to ESPNcricinfo

No, I wouldn't consider myself the GOAT of cricket. For me, only two people qualify for it. It's Sachin Tendulkar and Viv Richards.

—Virat Kohli on Sachin Tendulkar to
***Star Sports,* 28 October 2022**

Growing up when I was your age, I used to watch him play and always thought I wanted to play like him but couldn't. Inside in my heart I always wanted to play like him, he was a cricketing idol growing up.

—M.S. Dhoni on Sachin Tendulkar
in an interview in October 2022

I played 122 Tests alongside Sachin, I never threatened his place as a batsman but he threatened mine as a bowler.

—Anil Kumble on Sachin Tendulkar on
13 November 2013 in an interview

Once, Sachin Tendulkar was out bowled. He said I saw the (ball) in the outswing and then it came inside. So, it was not my fault, the balls were exchanged. That was not even an excuse, it was a genuine reason. I said only a God can see that, Tendulkar is God himself. More so, because this never happened in our lives.

—Virender Sehwag on
The Kapil Sharma Show

Opponents

DAVID WARNER

Each of us who played cricket in this era grew up admiring Sachin Tendulkar. He was like a benchmark of sorts. Everything great about our sport was associated with him. As a youngster growing up in Australia and dreaming of scoring international centuries, I used to look at Sachin Tendulkar with a sense of awe! A hundred international hundreds and 35,000 runs in international cricket it does appear surreal on occasions. How is it even possible! And when you add that he played the sport at the highest level for 24 years, you are like, this man is a genius.

Most importantly, he played for India. A country where cricketers are demigods put on a pedestal if they do well but severely criticised if they don't. With a billion people watching the sport day in and out, the pressure the Indian cricketers play with every day is unreal. For Sachin, the pressure was more than anyone. He was expected to perform every single time he walked out to bat. Every action of his was scrutinised, and every single move was decoded and analysed repeatedly on television. In fact, as I have said on many occasions, if one has a career which is half as good as his, one should be delighted. I would go a step further and say if one has a career a third as good as his, he'd have done his country proud.

To survive at the top of the game for nearly two-and-a-half decades and play under the kind of pressure Sachin has, there is little doubt that he is the best most of us have seen or are likely to see in the future. He had success in every part of the world and is perhaps the only non-Australian cricketer who was given a standing ovation in all Australian cricket grounds. The Australian public loved everything he did, which is a tribute to his achievements over 24 long years. We in Australia love to play our sport hard. And it takes work to win us over. We are a competitive lot, and for anyone who plays in Australia, we would throw everything we got at him. And only if you pass the Test do we warm up to you. Sachin scored a hundred against Australia at 19 at the WACA on one of the fastest pitches in world cricket. He scored a hundred at the MCG in a Boxing Day Test, which we always aspired to do. It meant the world to me when I got to a double hundred in my 100th Test in front of an MCG crowd. For Sachin, who only toured Australia every three or four years, to score a hundred in a Boxing Day Test is an exceptional achievement. When you see his record at the SCG, it is among the best ever. For example, the innings of 241 not out in Steve Waugh's retirement Test is a lesson for every cricketer who plays the sport. To rein himself in for 641 minutes and not play the stroke you love to play is simply unreal. It takes the kind of patience that few can ever dream of having and shows a mental steel every sportsperson would feel privileged to have.

I did not know him well enough before the 2013 series against India, and I still can't say I do. The truth is I still look at him with a sense of reverence. However, when I approached him for his signed shirt, Sachin happily obliged. In fact, he asked me to see him at the end of the Delhi Test in 2013 and gave me one of his shirts, which I now treasure. It was easily the best gift to carry back home from India.

Since then, I have met him many times and interacted with him a few times. But I am still in awe. How can a man be as good as he was? How can you do the things he did for a good 24 years?

When I was asked to write for this special volume, the first question I asked myself was, what is the one thing about Sachin that stands out the most for me? The answer is his passion for the game. We could see it each time he stepped out onto the field. He has been one of the game's greatest ambassadors, and I hope he continues to serve cricket for many more years. The loudest cheer was reserved for him during the 2015 World Cup prize distribution ceremony at the MCG.

Each time I have felt pressure, I have thought back to him. How did he negotiate the pressure a billion people put on him? What all did he do and yet never looked flustered? How did he keep scoring runs by the heap when the crowd kept shouting Sachinn Sachinnn after every ball he faced?

The other important thing is he was a multi-format cricketer. While he did not play much T-20 cricket, which wasn't as popular then, all you need to do is see some of his innings, and you know he could be as successful in the format if he did. To play six World Cups and be the highest scorer in two of them and the second highest in one, his was a career that can never be emulated. I will be playing the IPL in India at the time of his 50th birthday and wish that I get an opportunity to personally wish him and celebrate with him. Sachin, wish you a very happy 50th birthday and your family all the good health and joy in the months and years ahead.

MICHAEL CLARKE

Firstly, I have the very highest regard for Sachin Tendulkar. Anyone who has achieved what he has and has continued to perform at the highest level for the amount of time he has will be remembered as one of the special people to have played cricket. He is our generation's best cricketer, and it has been a privilege playing with and against him. Longevity and consistency, I have always maintained, are hallmarks of greatness, and Sachin best exemplifies these qualities among contemporary cricketers.

People may not know that on my debut series in India in 2004, Sachin presented me with a pair of gloves. He had signed them for me, and they have pride of place in my trophy cabinet maintained by my grandfather in Sydney.

Though he has scored many runs against Australia and has played some of his best knocks against us, I have always enjoyed seeing him bat. Competing against the very best offers a different level of excitement, and that's what it has been like playing against Sachin for nearly a decade.

When you have achieved Sachin's amount, it is easy to let your guard down. But Sachin's uniqueness was his ability to keep the intensity going even after 24 years of international cricket. He chased every ball hard, ran every single run with intensity, and appealed with great passion, and every young star should learn from him.

In cricket, we speak a lot about technique. How is a batsman as good as he is? It is due to two things. First is his technique, and the second is his mental strength. There has been no better player with a better technique than Sachin Tendulkar. And when you add his mental strength to this, you will know you speak of an exceptional cricketer. When he batted against us, we felt it was impossible to get him out. It was as if he was batting with a wooden door in his hand rather than a cricket bat. His bat was much wider than it actually is, and this is because of his technique. For example, some of the straight drives he played can only be played if you have a technique he did. Not without reason do I say he was the best player of our era.

Now add to this the pressure he played under. India is the most passionate country when it comes to cricket. It has a legion of fans who look at its cricketers as demigods. And Sachin was a class above. Fans expected the world from him each time he stepped out on the park. They knew he was capable. He had done it time and again. 100 international centuries over 24 years. In front of fans who would keep celebrating him with Sachin Sachin chants.

Century No 1: 119 not out vs England at
Old Trafford, on Aug 14, 1990

Century No 2: 148 not out India vs
Australia at Sydney, on Jan 6, 1992

Century No 3: 114 vs Australia at Perth, on
Feb 3, 1992

Century No 4: 111 vs South Africa at
Johannesburg, on Nov 28, 1992

Century No 5: 165 vs England at Chennai,
on Feb 12, 1993

Century No 6: 104 not out vs Sri Lanka at Colombo,
on Jul 31, 1993

Century No 7: 142 vs Sri Lanka at Lucknow,
on Jan 19, 1994

Century No 8: 110 vs Australia, at Colombo,
on Sep 9, 1994 (FIRST IN ODIS)

Century 10: 105 vs West Indies at Jaipur,
on Nov 11, 1994

Century No 9: 115 vs New Zealand at
Vadodara, on Oct 28, 1994

Century No 11: 179 vs West
Indies at Nagpur, on Dec 2, 1994

Century No 12: 112 not out vs Sri Lanka
at Sharjah, on Apr 9, 1995

Century No 13: 127 not out vs Kenya at
Cuttack, on Feb 18, 1996

Century No 14: 137 vs Sri Lanka at New Delhi,
on Mar 2, 1996

Century No 15: 100 vs Pakistan at
Padang, on Apr 5, 1996

Century No 16: 118 vs Pakistan at
Sharjah, on Apr 15, 1996

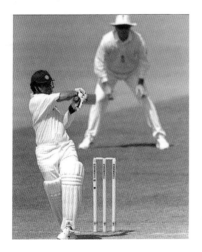

Century No 17: 122 vs England at
Birmingham, on Jun 8, 1996

Century No 18: 177 vs England at Nottingham,
on Jul 5, 1996

Century No 19: 110 vs Sri Lanka at Colombo, on
Aug 28, 1996

Century No 20: 114 vs South Africa
at Mumbai, on Dec 14, 1996

Century No 21: 169 vs South Africa
at Cape Town, on Jan 4, 1997

Century No 22: 104 vs Zimbabwe
at Benoni, on Feb 9, 1997

Century No 23: 117 vs New
Zealand at Bangalore, on May
14, 1997

Century No 24: 143 vs Sri Lanka at
Colombo, on Aug 3, 1997

Century No 25: 139 vs Sri Lanka at
Colombo, on Aug 11, 1997

Century No 26: 148 vs Sri Lanka at Mumbai, on Dec 4, 1997

Century No 27: 155 not out vs Australia at Chennai, on Mar 9, 1998

Century No 28: 177 vs Australia at Bangalore, on Mar 26, 1998

Century No 29: 100 vs Australia at Kanpur, on Apr 7, 1998

Century No 30: 143 vs Australia at Sharjah, on Apr 22, 1998

Century No 31: 134 vs Australia at Sharjah, on Apr 24, 1998

Century No 32: 100 not out vs Kenya at Kolkata,
on May 31, 1998

Century No 33: 128 vs Sri Lanka at
Colombo, on Jul 7, 1998

Century No 34: 127 vs Zimbabwe at
Bulawayo, on Sep 26, 1998

Century No 35: 141 vs Australia at Dhaka,
on Oct 28, 1998

Century No 36: 118 not out vs
Zimbabwe at Sharjah, on Nov 8, 1998

Century No 37: 124 vs Zimbabwe at
Sharjah, on Nov 13, 1998

Century No 38: 113 vs New Zealand at
Wellington, on Dec 29, 1998

Century No 39: 136 vs Pakistan at Chennai,
on Jan 31, 1999

Century No 40: 124 not out vs Sri Lanka at
Colombo, on Feb 28, 1999

Century No 41: 140 vs Kenya at
Bristol, on May 23, 1999

Century No 42: 120 vs Sri Lanka at
Colombo, on Aug 29, 1999

Century No 43: 126 not out vs New
Zealand at Mohali, on Oct 13, 1999

Century No 44: 217 vs New Zealand at Ahmedabad, on Oct 30, 1999

Century No 45: 186 vs New Zealand at Hyderabad, on Nov 8, 1999

Century No 46: 116 vs Australia at Melbourne, on Dec 28, 1999

Century No 48: 101 vs Sri Lanka at Sharjah, on Oct 20, 2000

Century No 47: 122 vs South Africa at Vadodara, on Mar 17, 2000

Century No 49: 122 vs Zimbabwe at New Delhi, on Nov 21, 2000

Century No 50: 201 not out vs Zimbabwe at Nagpur, on Nov 26, 2000

Century No 51: 146 vs
Zimbabwe at Jodhpur, on
Dec 8, 2000

Century No 52: 126 vs Australia at Chennai,
on Mar 20, 2001

Century No 53: 139 vs Australia at
Indore, on Mar 31, 2001

Century No 54: 122 vs West Indies
at Harare, on Jul 4, 2001

Century No 55: 101 vs South Africa at
Johannesburg, on Oct 5, 2001

Century No 56: 146 vs Kenya at Paarl,
on Oct 24, 2001

Century No 57: 155 vs South Africa at
Bloemfontein, Nov 3, 2001

Century No 58: 103 vs
England at Ahmedabad, on
Dec 13, 2001

Century No 59: 176 vs Zimbabwe at Nagpur, on
Feb 24, 2002

Century No 60: 117 vs West
Indies at Port of Spain,
on Apr 20, 2002

Century No 61: 105 vs England at
Chester-Le-Street, on Jul 4, 2002

Century No 62: 113 vs Sri Lanka at Bristol,
on Jul 11, 2002

Century No 63: 193 vs England at Leeds,
on Aug 23, 2002

Century No 64: 176 vs West Indies at Kolkata,
on Nov 3, 2002

Century No 65: 152 vs Namibia at
Pietermaritzburg, on Feb 23, 2003

Century No 66: 100 vs Australia at
Gwalior, on Oct 26, 2003

Century No 68: 241 not out vs Australia at Sydney,
on Jan 4, 2004

Century No 67: 102 vs New
Zealand at Hyderabad,
on Nov 15, 2003

Century No 69: 141 vs Pakistan at
Rawalpindi, on Mar 16, 2004

Century No 70: 194 not out vs
Pakistan at Multan,
on Mar 29, 2004

Century No 71: 248 not out
vs Bangladesh at Dhaka, on
Dec 12, 2004

Century No 72: 123 vs Pakistan at Ahmedabad,
on Apr 12, 2005

Century No 73: 109 vs Sri Lanka at
New Delhi, on Dec 22, 2005

Century No 74: 100 vs Pakistan at Peshawar,
on Feb 6, 2006

Century No 75: 141 not out vs West Indies
at Kuala Lumpur, on Sep 14, 2006

Century No 76: 100 not out vs
West Indies at Vadodara,
on Jan 31, 2007

Century No 77: 101 vs Bangladesh in
Chittagong, on May 19, 2007

Century No 79: 154 not out vs Australia at Sydney,
on Jan 4, 2008

Century No 78: 122 not out vs
Bangladesh at Mirpur, on May 26, 2007

Century No 80: 153 vs Australia at
Adelaide, on Jan 25, 2008

Century No 81: 117 not out
vs Australia at Sydney, on Mar 2, 2008

Century No 83: 103 not out vs England at Chennai,
on Dec 15, 2008

Century No 82: 109
vs Australia at Nagpur, on Nov
6, 2008

Century No 85: 160 vs New
Zealand at Seddon Park,
on March 20, 2009

Century No 84: 163 vs New Zealand at
Christchurch, on Mar 8, 2009

Century No 86: 138 vs Sri Lanka at
Colombo, on Sep 14, 2009

Century No 87: 175
vs Australia at Hyderabad,
on Nov 5, 2009

Century No 88: 100 not out
vs Sri Lanka at Ahmedabad, on
Nov 20, 2009

Century No 89: 105 not out
vs Bangladesh at Chittagong,
on Jan 18, 2010

Century No 90: 143 vs
Bangladesh at Mirpur, on
Jan 25, 2010

Century No 91: 100 vs South Africa at Nagpur,
on Feb 9, 2010

Century No 92: 106 vs South Africa at Kolkata,
on Feb 15, 2010

Century No 93: 200 not out vs South
Africa at Gwalior, on Feb 24, 2010

Century No 94: 203 vs Sri Lanka at Colombo,
on Jul 28, 2010

Century No 95: 214
vs Australia at Bangalore, on Oct
11, 2010

Century No 96: 111 not out vs South
Africa at Cape Town, on Dec 19, 2010

Century No 97: 146 vs South
Africa at Cape Town, on Jan 4, 2011

Century No 98: 120 vs England at Bangalore, on
Feb 27, 2011

Century No 99: 111 vs South Africa at
Nagpur, on Mar 12, 2011

Century No 100: 114 vs Bangladesh at Mirpur,
on Mar 16, 2012

Having played the game and captained Australia, I can tell you it's challenging. You need to have nerves of steel to be able to perform under such pressure of expectations. To not feel overawed. Daunted. Sachin did so every single day of his career. He stayed true to the sport and finally achieved what he wanted to accomplish all through—winning the world cup. He is a story for us all to learn from.

To conclude, it has been a privilege playing against him, and I wish him all the best for his 50th birthday. But, most importantly for all of us in the sport, he has enriched Test cricket, the pinnacle of our much-loved game.

SOURASHISH LAHIRI

Like all youngsters growing up in our generation, Sachin was like God to most of us. There was a Coke ad with the tagline Eat Cricket, Drink Cricket, Sleep Cricket. For me, cricket was Tendulkar. So I used to switch off my TV set when he got out.

Meeting him (Sachin) for the first time was an excellent experience. I was selected in the India B side for Challenger Trophy in Chennai. I remember meeting him before the match as both teams were having lunch before leaving for the stadium. Dadi (Sourav) was also in the same team as me.

It was a memorable experience playing against the man I considered my role model. He scored a hundred and got out to me in that match. He looked tired after reaching the three-figure mark because of the humid conditions in Chennai and got out trying to hit me over mid-wicket. To have Sachin Tendulkar against the wickets column meant the world to me. I could tell generations that I had got the great Sachin Tendulkar out.

The next time I played against the master was in a Ranji Trophy final. I was fortunate to get him twice in that match. The night before the final, we all (Deep Dasgupta, Ranadeb Bose, Abhishek Jhunjhunwala, Rohan Gavaskar and Manoj Tiwari) discussed how to get Sachin out. We also discussed how we should celebrate when we get him out. I didn't imagine I would be the one. Manoj and Abhishek were surprised by my low-key celebration. He was caught at mid-wicket by Laxmi. He tried to hit me over the covers in the second innings and was again caught brilliantly by Laxmi. It was a fantastic feeling to have him in each innings of the game.

However, he had already done the damage by the time he got out and won the final for Mumbai. In fact, he made batting look so easy that it was difficult to bowl to him. He was playing cautiously until a delivery from Dinda spurred him up. The ball hit the master on the helmet. What we witnessed after that was an exhibition of batsmanship with no parallel. It was all class and confidence. Deep Dasgupta, our captain, packed the off-side with a 7–2 field. But that hardly stemmed the run flow, and Sachin was still easily finding gaps and constantly sweeping me. He literally toyed with our bowling and scored a hundred. I realized why he was called the God of cricket and considered way above the rest.

I had no interaction with him after the match. I just shook hands with him. Frankly, that was enough. I was happy that I had got an opportunity to play in the Ranji Trophy final against Sachin. For me, life is cricket, and cricket is Sachin. On the cricket field, the master scored a hundred tons. In life as well, we want him to score a century. Happy birthday, Sachin.

Quotes from other opponents

Australia is a country where they love sportsmen of high quality, and I have no doubt that outside of India, you will find Tendulkar's greatest admirers among my countrymen. His centuries in Sydney and Perth in India's 1991–92 series, at age 19, ensured that his career would be one that all cricket lovers in Australia would follow closely. Interestingly, I did not witness either innings, but many of my teammates did swear that it was batsmanship of the highest quality—high praise for a bloke who had not celebrated his 20th birthday. By the time I made my international debut Tendulkar was already being counted among the best batsmen in the world. Most bowlers knew that his was the crucial wicket in an Indian batting line-up that boasted of many talented batsmen. I have never made a secret of the fact that I rate Tendulkar the best batsman in the business. As far as I am concerned he is technically the most sound player I have ever bowled to. Add to that the manner in which he plays, always trying to dominate the bowler.

—**Glenn McGrath in a column**

Overall when I talk about all-time batsmen, Sachin Tendulkar had a magnificent technique. When I was England skipper, I cannot remember how many team meetings we used to have just to discuss how to get Tendulkar out.

—Nasser Hussain on ICC cricket podcast

Sachin was calm and yet aggressive. If I would try and sledge him, he would get even more determined.

**—Wasim Akram on Aakash Chopra's
YouTube channel**

My first impression of Sachin was that I had never seen an Indian batsman so accomplished against extreme fast bowling. Indian batters were good against spin but here was a teenager who scored runs against the best teams, bowling attacks in the world. From that day, I measured myself against Sachin. He was a few miles ahead of me at that time, I really wanted to be on par with him.

**—Brian Lara on Sachin Tendulkar at the
HT Leadership Summit 2022**

We did think for a while that he had a weakness with the ball coming back in through the gate driving on the up. We got him out a couple of times so maybe we could get him out playing the cover drive. That was our plan in Sydney and he refused to play a cover drive and got 241 not out. So it just shows he can adapt his game and overcome the plans of the opposition.

—Steve Waugh

Beyond Cricket

ABHINAV BINDRA

I have always been a Sachin Tendulkar fan. In fact, my cricket watching was centred around Sachin. I grew up watching him and have stopped watching cricket since he retired. Growing up wanting to play sports, Sachin was someone we all looked up to. I remember meeting him in 1998 during the Commonwealth Games, and I still have fond memories. Shooting was in Langkawi, and we had come to KL for the opening ceremony. As a 15-year-old, it was a complete fanboy moment. 1998 was one of Sachin's best years, and to see him up close was an extraordinary moment for me.

In my own career, I had always tried to retain the childlike enthusiasm for the sport till the last day I competed. Unless you have that, you won't be able to sustain yourself at the top for an extended period. That's what Sachin was able to do. He played at the highest level with distinction for a good 24 years. Now you can't do that unless you are deeply passionate about the sport and retained your childlike enthusiasm and passion for it when you started.

Yes, your approach towards the game could change. In fact, it will change, for change is the only constant in life, but the passion for the sport is never dimmed. That's what stands out for Sachin.

He wanted to win a World Cup for India and wasn't willing to give up till he fulfilled his dream. And it took him 22 years to do so. You can never do this if you aren't passionate about the sport. And while there were substantial external pressures on him to deliver, I am sure there were internal pressures too. He must have felt the force of his own conscience based on the high standards he had set. You have your own expectations of yourself, and such internal pressures aren't easy to deal with for any athlete. In sports, you must come to terms with the fact that you will fail occasionally. Fail more than you will succeed. You will not always win a tournament. But then you have to pick yourself up and give it your best day in and day out. To be able to do so for the time Sachin did shows how committed he was to the sport, and that's a lesson for every aspiring sportsperson.

In a long career, you are bound to have injuries and lows. Sachin, too had his share. From my experience, such things can be draining. But then you can't let negativity get the better of you. In his case, he was always able to come out of these situations because he was true to his sport. To win a World Cup after 22 years of effort is the testimony.

It is also about how you conduct yourself. Self-awareness is always the key. To score 100 international centuries tells you Sachin always lived in the present. Was acutely conscious of what was expected of him and delivered time and again in critical situations. With millions watching him, you can understand how difficult it must have been. And that's why he will forever be a role model for sportsmen and sportswomen worldwide.

A World Cup comes every four years in cricket, much like the Olympics. But then, to be able to do well, you must train every day, leading to the World Cup, for days, months, and years. For me, the Olympic games did not come every four years. It came every day. Preparation was always the key. I trained every day and was about trying to get the process right. At the end of the day, when I stood in front of the mirror and asked myself if I had given it my best and if the answer was yes, I would sleep well with a smile. That's what stood out about Sachin. He was prepared to give it his best each time he stepped out. Day in and day out. You could see that in his actions until the last day he played. When he stepped out and worshipped the pitch the day he retired, you clearly understood what it meant to him. He lived the sport for the entire duration he played, and to be able to do so for 24 years is phenomenal.

Finally, success, too, comes with its own share of crises. When you win an Olympic gold or a World Cup or score that many hundreds, the question is, what next? For years what you wanted and strived for, you have achieved. How do you keep motivating yourself and do things all over again? How do you sustain the same intensity once you have fulfilled your dream? And at the same time, stay humble and honest. That's the best part about Sachin. No achievement unfazed him. He could do things over and over again and burn his past. Anyone who wishes to play the sport should see his career as a life lesson. He would score hundreds, win matches for India, be the best player on many occasions and yet move on to the next challenge without thinking much about the past. He could keep the motivation level up all through. That's why he could have a career like the one he did.

As he turns 50, I wish him a very happy and healthy birthday and the family all the best. While we don't get to meet that often, suffice it to say I am a Sachin Tendulkar fan and will always remain so. And Sachin will always be a role model, one who will be the idol for millions who take to the sport. Seeing him play has been a pleasure, and each time I have met him has been a privilege.

PULLELA GOPICHAND

When you play a sport, you start out with the same goal—
to be the best in the sport you play. In my sport, Prakash
sir was the only example I had in front of me in India.
But he had played the sport before I came on the scene,
and the connection was distant. So it was natural I would
look somewhere else for inspiration. For example, we did
not have a world-beater in badminton in the late 80s. No
one believed we could win at the world stage. We weren't
even competitive to start with. And that's where Sachin
became relevant to me. He was that inspiration as far as I was
concerned. Here was an Indian athlete who could dominate
his sport in a manner no one had before. He was able to
script extraordinary feats repeatedly against the world's best
bowlers and do things for India for years and years. I did not
have to go far to look for inspiration. I just had to look at
Sachin. He was the embodiment of all that was good about
sport. Discipline, hard work, dedication and passion. All I
needed to do was imbibe from him. If he could, so could

I. We in India can produce the world's best sportsmen and women, and here is a living example.

I may not have known Sachin well. In fact, the truth is while growing up, I hardly knew him at all. And yet he was there. Each time he stepped on the field against Australia and scored runs, it reinforced a belief that all of us were after. That we in India can produce champions. That we can perform against the best in the world and win. And yet when you see him, he stayed rooted. He stayed modest and humble. No achievement got to him. There was a kind of quality about him that endeared him to many. That's what I needed to learn from him, and I tried to.

I don't need to tell you how good Sachin was. Who am I to try and understand his game and tell you he was the best batsman in the world. His record is for all of us to see. To play for 24 years and score 100 international centuries says it all. The runs he has scored are all etched in people's consciousness in India. I am interested in telling you how Sachin had moulded consciousness even when he had no idea he was doing so. We did not play the same sport. Never met. And yet he was there as a beacon of hope and a kind of role model. He was the representative of us all at the international level. For example, when I played and won the All-England, I had to believe I could do it. That I could be the best. That's where Sachin made a difference to us all.

The other thing I want to talk about is dealing with injuries. I suffered many injuries during my career and had to undergo multiple operations to keep playing. Eventually, I had to give up playing because it was impossible to deal with injuries. Each time you get injured, and it will happen to everyone who plays sport at the highest level, the comeback is hard. It is a continuous challenge. Mentally and physically. Apprehensions start to creep in, and you begin to question yourself. There is often a disconnect between body and mind. You feel scared. That's where Sachin is unique. He had so many injuries in his career and had to undergo so many surgeries, yet each time he returned stronger. At no point did he feel he couldn't stage a comeback. And keep getting better and better. This is a quality I haven't seen in anyone. His ability to overcome injuries and come back stronger tells me two things. First, he is mentally very strong. And second, he loved the sport far more than anything else. No injury could get him down. Nothing really mattered to him more than his love of playing the sport. His zeal to wear the Indian jersey helped him overcome every adversity thrown at him.

Few can do this, for it is the hardest thing to do. Also, when you think of Sachin's career, let's accept that sports science wasn't as good as it is now. Things weren't as advanced. Recovery was harder, and many succumbed to injuries as a result. Sachin did not and kept fighting. And this was a battle that he alone was fighting. Away from people and public glare. With his own internal self. And each time, he won. Trust me when I say this is as hard as winning any tournament and scoring any century. Every person who plays sport should learn this from him. To love the sport so much that no injury can push you back after a point.

Finally, I would like to take this opportunity to thank Sachin for all that he has done for us all and for enriching Indian and world sport. As someone who has conducted himself with dignity and honour, he will forever stay a role model for millions of sports fans in India. As he turns 50 and celebrates an unbeaten half-century, I wish him a 101st century and a life more fulfilling in the years to come. Happy birthday and God bless.

YOHAN BLAKE

Growing up in our part of the world in Jamaica, cricket was all about two men. Brian Lara and Sachin Tendulkar. While most of my mates were Brian fans, I had a massive affinity for Sachin since I was a 4-year-old child. There was something about him that I just loved, and it only grew over time. Wherever I travelled to compete during my career, I'd always try and follow Sachin bat if there was a game he was playing in. It had become a kind of routine for me.

However, the one story I must share is what happened when he scored the first-ever ODI double hundred. We were at a pub in Jamaica, and I was the only one who predicted that he could get to the magic 200 mark for the first time in cricket history. None of my mates agreed, and we ended up having a bet. If he did get to 200, they would take me out to dinner, and we would then party all night.

As he scored 200, I was thrilled. I had just earned a lovely dinner, and if I had his number, I would have called him to say thank you. I have been a Sachin Tendulkar fan growing up, and my adulation for him has been a constant throughout my career.

As I started to do well in my career, I had the opportunity to know him. And each time I have spoken to him, it has been a special feeling. He is looked upon as God in India, yet he is the most humble person you can come across. I loved what I saw when I was in India for the Tata Mumbai Marathon in January 2023. People love their sport and make us athletes feel really special. If I could receive the kind of love and affection I did during my visit, I can well imagine what Sachin is like to his fans in India. Such love makes you feel blessed, which is a huge thing for anyone.

The one thing I want to point out here, which brings Sachin closer to me, is his work ethic. I have always worked the hardest in training. Never did I resort to any shortcut. I trained for hours and hours and was determined to be the best version of myself. That's what every athlete should train for. Sachin has always spoken about this in his career. There is no substitute for hard work; you must be disciplined and committed to your sport. He ruled his sport for over two decades, demonstrating his work ethic and discipline.

As he turns 50, I wish him a very happy birthday and look forward to catching up with him soon. Each time you meet him, you come away with something special, and I am sure it will be no different this time around. And we will celebrate his 50th when we meet!

DEVENDRA JHAJHARIA

For me, sport is all about respect. The respect you earn and the respect you give a fellow sportsperson. Even if you are hugely successful and yet you don't accord respect to other fellow sportspersons, you can't be a role model in my eyes. Far more than sporting success, what is important is how you are as a human being and your values. And that's where Sachin Tendulkar stands out. Despite being the greatest player ever, he treats every sportsperson respectfully, making them feel welcome.

Soon after I won the Rio 2016 gold medal, the second Paralympic gold of my career, Sachin Tendulkar organised a reception for us in Mumbai. He had done so for the Olympic medal winners, and the felicitation of para-athletes was done with no less grandeur. All the medal winners and athletes who had missed the medal by a whisker were also present. Sachin was present the whole time and interacted with each one of us. I remember a fascinating conversation with him over the use of theraband. I had done a lot of theraband exercises ahead of the Rio games, which had helped me immensely. It helped strengthen the shoulder and the elbow, and when I mentioned it to Sachin, he said he, too, had used the theraband a lot towards the end of his career. We then discussed the importance of scientific training and how proper training modules can significantly impact an athlete's career.

Thereafter I met Sachin again during the inauguration of the Fanattic Sports Museum in Kolkata, and he said something I will never forget in my life. He said while we all do events and it is an integral part of all our lives, never should we do an event at the expense of our sport. We should never miss any training session for an event. Sport, he said, always comes first, and this statement of his has stayed with me ever since.

During the museum inauguration, Boria ji asked Sachin to do the honours and formally cut the ribbon. As his biographer, it was natural for Boria ji to do so. Sachin, however, changed the whole thing around. He was helping Deepa Malik with her wheelchair and asked Deepa to cut the ceremonial ribbon. For a para-athlete to do so in the presence of luminaries like Sachin, Abhinav and Sourav Ganguly meant a lot to us all. It was a coming together of able-bodied and para sports, and Sachin was responsible for making it happen.

As someone who has fought for equal treatment of able-bodied and para-athletes, Sachin will always have a special place for me. It is because he is a true ambassador of the cause and practices it in his life. So to conclude, I am a huge Sachin Tendulkar fan and a proud one. Will always look up to Sachin as an idol of mine and one of the best India has ever produced.

VISHWANATHAN ANAND

Sachin and I burst into the sports scene almost simultaneously, and thereafter our careers have had very similar trajectories. Even today, there are several similarities. While I continue to play the sport for enjoyment rather than for any career goal, Sachin, too, is doing the same and playing certain tournaments. This is because of his love for the sport. Cricket is all he knows, and for someone as dedicated and passionate, it is near impossible to completely give it up.

With Sachin in the 1990s, there was something unique. Almost everyone in India would call him by his first name, and a deep affection was attached to it. He was like the son in every Indian household we identify with. He was the answer to every Indian problem in cricket and was always the boy next door. He wasn't a superstar. He was one of our own. One we identified with. Cared for. Loved. And the best thing about him is he could retain this boy next door image till the very last day of his career.

What brought both our careers together in a way is the

longevity. While I played for a good three decades, Sachin played for 24 years. If you play for so long, there is only one answer. You just want to play the sport more than anything else. The passion for it is undiminished even after 20-plus years, and each time you play, there is a joy difficult to put down in words.

The other thing similar is the wait for the world title. Sachin waited for 22 years before he finally laid his hands on the World Cup. We in chess waited a long time before winning the Chess Olympiad. Winning in a team sport is very different compared to winning individually. And when you play as a team for India, there is a very different connotation attached. To be the best in your sport as a team is a dream, and Sachin pursued this dream with unwavering focus and passion. I watched every game of the 2011 World Cup and felt very happy for Sachin when India won the trophy. It was a dream fulfilled, and no one deserved it more.

While I am three years older, I am also a fan of his and his conduct. With such adulation all around him, he has managed to stay grounded and has never lost his humility. And in both our cases, we are very Indian. We are deeply attached to our families and are invested in Indian traditions while taking great pride in doing what we do for our country. So on the occasion of his 50th birthday, I wish him and the family a lot of good health and happiness and hope that he continues to fulfil all his dreams in the years ahead.

DEEPA MALIK

Rio 2016 changed it all. All of a sudden, I was a celebrity. Having won the first-ever paralympic silver medal for India as a woman, I was inundated with interview requests on my return from Rio. Never before had such a thing happened to me. Everywhere I went, people asked for selfies and autographs. It was daunting. From a normal person who played sport, this was a life I wasn't used to. Each word was measured, and each statement was decoded deeply. That's when Sachin called us to Mumbai for a felicitation. He was generous enough to call all the Paralympic medal winners to Mumbai for a grand felicitation, which he had organised. And with Sachin, everything is of scale. The media was there in numbers, and everyone wanted a piece of him. Yet he was never flustered. It was all very natural and normal. He was kind and polite with everyone, listened to everyone and interacted with us all for hours. The way he conducted himself was a real-life lesson for me. He labelled us athletes with extraordinary abilities and celebrated us through the programme.

When I think that continued media attention is every day for Sachin, I realise what it must have taken for him to mould himself in the manner he has. Each word he says is news. Everything he does is followed by millions in the country and beyond. And yet he has stayed rooted. Humble and modest. That's the biggest learning from him. How to conduct yourself in public and endear yourself to people. That's what I have tried to do every single day of my life. Conduct myself with dignity and be polite and gracious to everyone around.

The other instance I want to recount here happened in Kolkata during the inauguration of the Fanattic Sports Museum in January 2017. Sachin, Sourav, Abhinav, Devendra and I were invited to the opening, and the organisers had requested Sachin to cut the ceremonial ribbon. Sachin, however, thought otherwise. He was actually pushing my wheelchair when the request was made and said to me that I should do the honours and handed me the scissor. I did not know what to do or say. In a moment, he had brought the world of able-bodied and para-sport together. He demolished every barrier that exists and ended every form of discrimination. As para-athletes, we have always fought for equality, which may be an ongoing struggle. However, it is something that will forever be our ultimate ambition. With Sachin, it was given. We were all equal. By allowing me to cut the ribbon, he made a statement. Frankly, it showed him as a person more than anything. If there is ever a role model in Indian sport, it has to be him.

Today, as he turns 50, I want to say a heartfelt thank you for all he has done for us in sports. He continues to inspire me and will always be a hero of mine. Happy birthday Sachin.

MANSI JOSHI

Dream on. Dreams do come true. Sachin always says this. For others, these may be words of encouragement. For me, however, they are much more. These words define my life in a way. When I was trying to return to sport and make a career out of it, these words were a constant source of support. As a para-athlete, I had my own share of challenges. Life wasn't easy. But that's what it is all about. To be able to fight. To overcome adversity. Dream on, as Sachin says. For dreams do come true. And may I say they have.

I have been a fan of Sachin since childhood. My sister and I used to play cricket, and growing up in Mumbai, it was natural that we would all be Sachin fans. We'd idolise him and try to emulate him. When I was in college, we had, as a group, bought tickets to go and watch Sachin play for the Mumbai Indians at Navi Mumbai. In fact, an entire stand was full of Sachin fans, and we were all screaming 'Sachinnn Sachinnn' right through the game. The following day we were a whole class of students who had lost their voices. It was funny.

All my growing up years, I have bought tickets to the Wankhede stadium to go and watch Sachin play. His batting was an addiction. You couldn't stay off it. You had to watch him bat to feel good. He was a balm for everything. If you felt down with something, all you needed to do was watch Sachin bat. Watching him play the straight drive was medicine. You had to smile. That's how relevant he was to all of us.

I continue to watch cricket whenever I can. But it has never been the same since Sachin retired. Like many in India, I was heartbroken when he decided to retire. He was a collective national yearning, and we were all part of this legion.

For a period, I felt I was one of his biggest fans. That there was none like me. However, when I went to the Wankhede to see him play, I realised how badly mistaken I was. There were many like me. In fact, many were bigger Sachin fans than I was. He was God to them. Literally and figuratively. Since then, I have never called myself his biggest fan, for there are others who are more passionate than I ever was.

But what Sachin has done for me and where he is different is that he has inspired me to become who I am. Play sports by overcoming all the challenges that life had thrown at me. Urged me to dream on for dreams do come true. So as I prepare for Paris 2024, the greatest stage of my life, Sachin's mantra will stay with me. I will continue to dream. For I know dreams do come true.

BHAVINA PATEL

I won the first Paralympics medal for India in Tokyo in 2021, and suddenly my life changed. I had never seen so many media people together, and to think they were all there for me was surreal. It was the same me who had once been told that I was a liability to the family because I had polio. And now, with the Paralympic medal around my neck, I was suddenly an achiever. For me, however, nothing had changed. I had worked the hardest to get to Tokyo. And then put in everything humanly possible to make India proud. The satisfaction of winning the medal was very personal, and I wanted to do something for myself. That's when Boria ji called my husband, and we got talking. He was a family friend, and Nikul asked me to tell him about my dream. He is Sachin sir's biographer and a good friend, and I remember telling him that my day would be complete if Sachin sir spoke to me for a couple of minutes. The whole country congratulated me on winning the medal, and Sachin sir had tweeted some very kind words. Only if I could speak to him once. As a fan, that's all I wanted.

Within 15 minutes, Boria ji called back and said he was getting Sachin sir on the line. He said Sachin sir had very happily agreed and had asked him to get us both on a conference call. That's when I heard, 'Hello Bhavina,' and I couldn't stop my emotions. Sachin Tendulkar, my hero, was at the other end of the line. As an athlete, there can be no greater achiever than him, and I had always hero-worshipped him while growing up. He congratulated me on winning the silver medal and spoke at length about the close semi-final I had won against the world's number 2 player. He said that if you work hard and dare to dream, dreams do come true. There is no substitute for hard work, and no shortcut can lead you to success. Frankly, I was still in a daze. For me, it had still not sunk in. It was none other than Sachin Tendulkar at the other end of the line, and I was fortunate enough to speak to him.

The conversation lasted 10 minutes, and in those 10 minutes, all Sachin sir did was inspire me. He was delighted and proud of what I had done and said he expected more from me in the future. Nothing else mattered. On a day when I had won the greatest medal of my life, my idol spoke to me on the phone for 10 minutes. After the call was over, Nikul and I literally pinched ourselves to check if all that was happening around us was for real. Sachin sir may never know what he means to us all in India. All I can say is he has inspired generations, and we will forever be in his debt. Wish him a very happy 50th birthday.

SANIA MIRZA

Grace under pressure

Sachin Tendulkar is one of the kindest sportsmen I know. He is all grace and dignity. I tweeted the same after he had wished me at the end of the Australian Open mixed doubles final.

To have consistently performed despite the pressure of a billion fans and more sets Sachin Tendulkar apart from the other sporting greats of the world. Few, if any, would have had to endure the ruthless, microscopic dissection of every move the man has made during his brilliant career spanning over 24 years. To have come out unscathed from this kind of relentless scrutiny on and off the field is a tribute, in itself, to the genius of Tendulkar.

As one who loves cricket and has followed the game since childhood, it's no surprise that I have grown up admiring him. There is a lot to learn from him. Absorb how to play sport at the highest level without getting overawed. How to deal with pressure and not get bogged down. How to stay mentally strong in the face of adversity. To step up under pressure and do it time and again for India. If there is, one thing we sportsmen and women want to learn is how to play well under pressure. Sachin is a living example of it. He is all about staying true to the sport. Everything else is irrelevant when you are in the middle. All you need to know at that point is why you are there. To play your sport and try and win the match for India. To win for the tricolour and for your fans. For yourself. That's what Sachin did for years.

My father is an ardent follower of the game, and cricket is ubiquitous in my life. It is the most watched and talked about sport in India, and each of Sachin's actions, as I said earlier, has been defined or devilled by a billion-plus for over 24 long years. However, the fact that he continues to inspire millions and be humble and modest is a testament to the man's character and values.

I would not be wrong in saying everyone has a little bit of Sachin in them. Each one of us was playing for him. Thinking with him. Walking out to bat with him. And yet when he played, there was always a sense of calm. A reassurance that everything was fine and would be so. He was this steadying influence on us all, and to think that a country of a billion could feel reassured by one man is a testimony to his genius.

I've been lucky enough to have encountered Sachin reasonably early. The first was when I was just 16 and had won the Junior Wimbledon doubles title. Sachin arranged for his signature Palio car to be presented to me. While he couldn't make it to the function, he called me at the time of the presentation, and there's little doubt I was more elated to speak to him than to have received my first car! He was Sachin Tendulkar, a childhood hero and one of the greatest to have played sport. To speak to him was a privilege.

The first time I met him was in a Hyderabad hospital, at a function arranged for the members of the medical fraternity. Both of us were guests on the occasion. Yet again, what stood out was Sachin's humility and modesty. He said to the doctors, 'My job of playing cricket is of very little significance compared to yours. I have the luxury of committing some errors in my field, but you are far more important and cannot afford to make a mistake in your job.'

Just read the words, and you will know here is someone who has his values in the right place. His conduct has been exemplary, and every aspiring youngster should take lessons from him. With the stardom he has enjoyed, it is easy to let things get into your head. To lose balance. Not so for Sachin. He has not changed a bit in the years I have known him.

The one salient thing that distinguishes Tendulkar from his contemporaries is the pressure we've put on him throughout his career. He was expected to score a ton every time he walked out to bat; anything less was considered unacceptable. The nation brooks no failure from Tendulkar. Having played an intensely competitive sport for over 18 years, I know what pressure can do to a sportsperson. It is often too much to bear for any of us. For Tendulkar, however, it appeared routine. This is what makes his achievements all the more daunting. To score 35,000 runs and 100 international centuries while playing with the kind of pressure he did is simply unthinkable. From being labelled a genius at a very early age to retiring at 40, Sachin always played with the kind of pressure that is insane. To think that 50,000 people would keep screaming your name each time you went out to bat is inconceivable. And yet it happened with Sachin time and again in India and all parts of the cricketing world.

Finally, I know what it takes to keep fit in high-performance sport. You must sacrifice many usual pleasures and maintain a strict work ethic all year round. Give up on the simple joys of life. And yet there are injuries. Injuries that leave you in pain and make you frustrated. It takes longer to get fit again and play at your best. Being able to do so when you're 40 and after putting the body through intense physical activity for 24 years couldn't have been easy. However, that's Sachin Tendulkar for you. Here's wishing India's biggest sporting icon a very happy 50th birthday.

Quotes from other sports stars

Why wait? I am ready to take notes.

—Roger Federer on Sachin Tendulkar's offer on exchanging notes on cricket and tennis after he cheekily played a forward defensive stroke at Wimbledon. This exchange had taken the social media world by storm.

Inner World

RAMAKANT ACHREKAR

He was barely three feet away from the TV screen, sitting on the edge of the bed in a red shirt and shorts following the action in the last Test of the India–Australia series. People kept coming and going, but his eyes didn't stray from the screen, taking in every detail.

Just a stone's throw away from the legendary Shivaji Park in Mumbai, we are seated in a 100 square feet drawing room in another of the city's unremarkable houses. What made it special was it was the residence of Ramakant Achrekar. There's very little sign of the famous alliance except for a solitary picture of Sachin standing behind his coach and a few friends at a far corner above the television, along with a miniature cricket bat.

At 80 years and four months, Achrekar sir was a man of few words. But talk to him about his favourite pupil, and the octogenarian made a serious attempt to speak.

This conversation occurred in March 2013, and we consider it fitting to reproduce it here. Ramakant Achrekar will always be a special person in Sachin Tendulkar's life.

'He continues to be the same, just as he was; there has been no change in him. He still visits me to seek my blessings. He constantly talks to me about cricket despite my limited speech,' said Achrekar sir.

'It's tough to distract father while he's watching a match,' added eldest daughter Vishakha, who was visiting.

Having just recovered from malaria, the Dronacharya awardee revealed that Sachin visited him before the Australia series to check on his health.

'While he discusses cricket, he spends a lot of time enquiring about my health. Even when he is on tour, he calls and speaks to my daughter Kalpana to stay updated. When they are in Mumbai, he and Anjali visit me often,' added Achrekar sir with a smile on his face as on the screen Sachin sprinted and returned the ball to the wicketkeeper from the boundary.

From taking Sachin on his own scooter to various grounds for matches to giving him a Re. 1 coin for remaining unbeaten, the Sachin–Achrekar story is captured in the annals of Indian cricket history. It is known to every cricket fan in India. During his early days, Sachin spent enough time at the Achrekar household to have developed a close bond with two of his daughters, Kalpana and Vishakha, who now run a cricket coaching centre. (In fact, even after his Test debut, they continued to compete in table tennis, and the story goes that Sachin was once defeated by them).

Kalpana, who stayed with her father, said, 'Sachin is

devoted to the game, and even after his retirement from ODIs he had spoken to baba (father).' Even at 80, cricket continued to be the dominant theme in Achrekar's life. 'He feels nice and really enjoys meeting people. He doesn't like sitting cooped up at home. We also drive down to Alibaug from Mumbai at times,' said Kalpana. There's an ad break in the match, so he turns back towards us as we speak to him about Sachin's birthday. A look of contentment on his face as he smiles broadly, 'Chikati Sodaychi nahin (Never leave your bat), I just want him to continue doing well and play for as long as he can.'

Despite his limited speech, as we grabbed the camera to take a picture, he stopped us from clicking and looked for his trademark brown cap. While his daughter found him a blue cap, he urged his grandson to look for his brown cap, put it on and gave a broad smile for a picture.

He called us back as we made our way out and signed off, 'Sachin should score a few more centuries.' Ramakant Achrekar, just like every Indian cricket fan, wanted his best pupil to wield magic with his willow forever.

SUNIL GAVASKAR

First, there was Sir Don Bradman, and then there was Sir Garfield Sobers.

Then it was Sachin Ramesh Tendulkar.

It's hard to believe that the then slightly chubby, baby-faced Sachin we saw in 1987 is going to complete 50 years. He is, of course, no longer chubby but finely muscled, but his face is still like a baby and even more so when he breaks into a smile.

Mumbai Cricket's grapevine is a legendary one. News of emerging talent spreads around the maidans and the Gymkhanas very fast. Then the curiosity factor kicks in as cricket followers, whatever their day jobs, find time to watch the name that is being whispered about almost reverentially. Once convinced, the whispers get louder, and soon the talk in all the street corners and kattas of the Gymkhanas is that a special one has arrived.

I had heard and read about Sachin's exploits at the school level but had not seen him play.

Hemant Waingankar, who sadly is no more, was like my younger brother, and he used to tell me at every opportunity how good a batter young Sachin was. So no wonder when he drove me to the airport to catch a flight to London for the Bi-Centenary Test match in 1987, the topic came to Sachin. Anil Joshi was also in the car and mentioned that the young man was a bit upset that he had not received the prestigious Best Junior Cricketer award that the then Bombay Cricket Association used to give annually at their awards evening. So as we arrived at the airport on impulse, I asked for a pen and then, on the bonnet of the car, wrote a letter to Sachin asking him not to get discouraged but to keep working hard. I also mentioned that one name was missing from the list of those who had won the awards previously, and that person hadn't done too badly in Test cricket.

A couple of months later, the Reliance World Cup happened, and that's when I met the young man for the first time. He was a ball boy for the tournament for the matches at the Wankhede Stadium, and I invited him to the sanctum santorum, the Indian dressing room and introduced him to the rest of the team.

I stopped playing after the tournament, and since he was the only young man using the super lightweight leg guards I used to prefer, I sent him mine as I didn't intend to play any cricket thereafter. A few days later, I went to the Wankhede Stadium to see him bat in the nets for the Mumbai Ranji Trophy probables. I watched from the dressing room since I didn't want him to feel conscious about being watched. I saw a batter with so much time to play the quicker bowlers that he could hit them on whichever side he wanted. I remember coming home and telling my wife I had seen a special talent that day. He, of course, was still a schoolboy cricketer and hadn't even played for Mumbai in the Ranji Trophy then. A couple of weeks later, when I came home from the office, my wife said, 'A young man is waiting for you; it must be the same guy you were talking about. He hasn't looked up and has been staring at his toes all this while.' It was indeed Sachin, and he had come to thank me for sending him the leg guards. He gave me a thank you card with his name written in block letters. I asked him to sign the card, and he scribbled a completely unreadable signature. I asked him if he had seen the signatures of Sir Don, Sir Garfield and even our own Vijay Merchant? I told him that even so many years after they retired, their signatures can be easily identified and that 50 years from now when fans look at autographs, they should be able to say, 'Ah, that's Sachin Tendulkar's autograph.' He nodded, and his next question floored me. He said, 'Yes, but isn't it easy to forge these signatures?' I couldn't help laughing, for a 14-year-old kid was conscious that his signature could be forged in the future.

Many years later, when my apartment got flooded while repair work was going on, I lost a lot of mementoes, and this card with its scribbled signature also got misplaced. But, of course, his signature can be easily made out today, and it's a huge thrill for cricket lovers to see it.

Having stopped playing and with more time on hand now, Hemant, Anil and I would watch him play wherever he was playing and cackle whenever he toyed with the bowlers. We thought he was our secret; only we knew how good he was and that he was ours. But of course, the cricketing world was waking up to the name, and so the three of us had to reluctantly accept that he now belonged to the cricketing world and not just us.

Hemant and Anil would keep me constantly updated on his scores, how he got them, who were the opposition bowlers, etc. We would not just talk about his batting but what he wore to functions, who he spoke with, etc. He used to only wear a white shirt folded to the elbows for the evening functions, and we used to discuss how he was so blandly dressed for a young kid. Then a couple of years later, Hemant called me excitedly and handed the phone to Anil, who, in his typical style, started, 'Sir, sir, sir, big news, sir, big news.' I waited, and then he said, 'Sir, Sachin wore a printed shirt for the function.' It was the first time he had given up the white shirt. We all laughed happily at the information, delighted that our boy was finally going to start dressing like a teenager and not in a boring white shirt.

He dresses impeccably now and even sends me some from his signature range. Hemant is no longer with us, but for Anil and me, somewhere down the line, we feel he is still our little boy who we should protect and look after. Mind you, we had zero contribution to his growth as a cricketer, but the sense that we saw and recognised his talent and potential makes us feel a sense of ownership.

He belongs to the cricketing universe now, and it's a matter of great pride and joy to see the love and affection with which he is treated wherever he goes. What's been admirable is how he has handled this mega success and remains so grounded.

There has never ever been a perfect cricketer or, for that matter, a perfect sportsperson, but Sachin comes closest to being the most perfect batter in the history of the game. Technically he made some changes to his back lift, pick up and follow-through.

Like golfers keep tweaking their swing, he also kept making little tweaks to his batting depending on the opposition and the pitch he was playing on. Along with Javed Miandad, the great Pakistani batter, Sachin has the sharpest cricketing mind with brimful of ideas to make the game a better one.

At 50, he has matured into a cricketing statesman, and if the authorities don't use his knowledge and experience, it will be the game's loss and not his. In Mumbai cricket, there is a tradition to give a newcomer a nickname, and we had given him the most unimaginative one, ' Tendlya'. Our 'Tendlya' is 50 now, and knowing his penchant for centuries, there's no doubt he will go on to score a century in life too.

Here's wishing him and his family the best today, tomorrow and always.

DR APARNA SANTHANAM

My friend Sachin

I first saw Sachin burst on the international cricket scene when I was in my late teens, a medical student who had been raised to be so cricket crazy that I would listen to the commentary and read newspaper articles on everything to do with cricket and even brave the dingy, smelly common room in the hostel to watch matches. I was no expert, but even I recognised it, as did people far wiser than me, that this young man was a genius, and we were watching the beginning of an epoch, not just in Indian cricket, but in sport and the world as a whole.

But the twist in the tale was yet to come. My best friend in the world, who, in many ways, defined the person and doctor I was becoming, fell dramatically in love with and started seeing Sachin. When your best friend gets serious about a boy, you undergo a serious conflict of emotions. You want to like him, but you are nervous he should be good enough for this remarkable person who is your person, and you are apprehensive about how your dynamics may change thanks to this relationship. So, it was with great excitement and cricketing awe, coupled with feelings of vague apprehensions and mistrust, that I met Sachin.

He was both diffident and disarming. With a mop of curly hair and a shy smile, he won me over instantly as I could sense he was not just smitten with Anjali but was nervous about meeting her friends. As a result, we developed a warm, cordial relationship based on genuine liking and a recognition that we were bound by the person who mattered so deeply to both of us. He was my best friend's husband. It was not until much later that he became my dear friend, too and in many ways, this independent relationship strengthened my bonds with Anjali even further.

I have so many stories in my head about Sachin. Do I talk about the evening when Anjali called saying come over, it's important, only to realise that he had decided to hang up his bat and boots, when we spent hours reminiscing, celebrating, popping champagne, determined we will not allow ourselves to be sad, staying up all night to celebrate his magnificence? Do I talk about his extreme kindness in dropping in unexpectedly, late at night, to see my parents who were feeling low and cheering them up by having dinner and hanging out with them? Do I talk about the prankster who revels in pulling practical jokes or the empathetic friend who is there for you without uttering a word? Do I talk about the expansive host who makes every outing fun or the foodie who loves fine cuisine as much as vada pav? Do I talk about the simple man who would rather sit at home, surrounded by the loyal friends of his childhood and youth, than grace the mega events that he is always invited to? Do I talk about the process of writing his autobiography that I was a part of, where in the narration of his story, we lived not just our life stories but the course of India over the 24 years he played? Do I talk about that moment of retirement at Wankhede stadium, listening to him talk? There was not a single dry eye in the crowd listening to him enraptured, knowing that this man, this moment a once-in-a-century event?

I will limit myself to two themes; the first is his humility; he will listen to your opinions on your expertise and your views on cricket as well. And what he cannot understand immediately, he has no qualms or hesitation in saying, 'I don't understand; please explain.' I remember sitting with him in Mussoorie, with a bunch of us all having opinions on his post-retirement life. He listened to everyone intently and then stated precisely what he wanted to do and what he did not. The humility, simplicity and utter clarity were just extraordinary.

The second aspect of his personality that few people know about is his sense of humour and ability to play pranks. The man is also a fantastic mimic and can easily transport you to fits of uncontrollable laughter. I remember, in London, sitting down on the sidewalk in the condo complex where they live, rolling with laughter as he was holding forth, and we were asked by the authorities to go home as we could not control our mirth at his poker-faced performance. I remember driving through Scotland with a kook ball of a driver, where he had us in splits over every shenanigan the driver came up with. Finally, I remember partnering with him in pulling a fast one on another friend and his uncontrollable joy when the prank actually played out exactly as planned!

Happy birthday dear friend. Your turning 50 is a landmark in all our lives, for a nation has watched you grow, bloom, and become more and more extraordinary, making us all a part of your journey year after year. So, here's wishing you the very best for all the bounty to come in the future years, to living a life that continues to be magical, purposive, exceptional and most of all, filled with the laughter and love of family and friends in just the ways that you want.

ATUL RANADE

My SRT at 50.

Since 1975, I have had the pleasure of knowing Sachin as a three-year-old cherubic boy in the kindergarten with long locks with whom I shared my tiffin (if not already devoured by him).

From there, to an enigmatic persona who not only garnered runs for 24 years but also earned the respect of India and the world as the flag-bearer every time he stepped out to bat for our country.

Someone who is loved and respected from Kashmir to Kanyakumari because of his conduct and down-to-earth attitude, Sachin is special.

Sachin is a family man, and family is always his priority. For example, when it comes to his mother, he gives attention to the minutest details regarding her well-being wherever he is. Apart from his vast input towards the charities he supports, I have seen him help his extremely close friends and teammates when in need or during any emergency.

On his 50th birthday, I would love to pray to our Ganpati Bappa to shower his blessings on my darling baby friend and give him the best of health.

JAGDISH CHAVAN

I saw blood-smattered gloves post-net session

I am 50 years old, just like Sachin Tendulkar. I started my cricketing journey at Shivaji Park Gymkhana, just like Sachin Tendulkar. Oh yes. I also appeared for trials at MRF Pace Foundation, just like Sachin Tendulkar. Well, the similarity just ends then and there. I am Jagdish Chavan, and to date, I have never had the inclination to tell my story. My Sachin Tendulkar story. Here I would.

Knowing him for more than two decades, what it meant to me, maybe co-ordinate training sessions for him, being the occasional net bowler and that insanely privileged fellow who was bestowed with the honour of serving the best cricketer in the world. I just count my blessings.

If cricket is an institution, Sachin will forever remain its best student. The most devoted one and blessed with unmatched acumen and powers of innovation. The practice sessions were like his preparation, full of purpose and intent.

The training session of Sachin was like a purohit sitting on a puja. He never trained for the heck of it. If there was a 6:30 am session the next day, he could send you a text at 1 am. 'Jagdish, please arrange a quality left-arm pacer and a leg spinner for tomorrow's session.' With Mumbai's club cricket producing a lot of quality and some good talent in the age group set-up, I could get him some good bowlers.

There were times when the pace he faced at the international level couldn't be matched by local youngsters, but Sachin even had a solution for that. Those who bowled at late 120s or early 130 clicks were told to overstep and send the ball from 17 to 18 yards, which would automatically ramp up the pace.

His homework would be precise and, at times, stun people like me that even after 130 odd Tests, he would be spending sleepless nights decoding bowlers and how to play them. I have a few treasured stories about Sachin and one I would never forget was his preparation to face Sohail Tanvir, the Pakistani left armer.

Now we all know that left-arm pacers will create awkward angles for right-handed batters, but Tanvir, with his wrong-footed action, made it double awkward as you only realised late which way the ball is moving.

One day as I entered MIG Club Bandra's indoor nets, I saw Sachin fiddling with the bowling machine. Initially, I thought he might be adjusting the speed, but then I saw that he was trying to change the angle of the front part from where the ball was released.

He wanted the ball machine to be kept at an angle and then wanted balls to be fed with the requisite swing so that he could simulate somewhat of what Tanvir was doing. In the monsoons, there would be times when he would ask me to provide throwdown on wet green patches with a wet tennis ball from 16 yards to cope with extreme pace.

The wet tennis balls from 16 yards can come at 150 clicks. Another time when Sachin had a wrist injury, I was with him when he went to check with the doctor. After his scan reports came, the doctor advised him against batting in the nets for the next 15 days as the impact of fast deliveries hitting the bat would hurt the wrist, and the injury would aggravate. Sachin always paid attention to medical advice as he took rehab and fitness seriously. But while coming down the stairs from the clinic, what he said stunned me.

'Jagdish, the doctor said not to hit balls, but there is no restriction on leaving deliveries, right? So from tomorrow until I can have nets, let's just practice leaving deliveries outside the off stump.' Well, I was speechless.

Another incident that made me laugh was before one of those Test tours of Sri Lanka, don't remember the year, though. It was an indoor session, and the staff knowing that Master would come for a session, had kept everything ready and adjusted the centralised AC to 24 degrees so that he felt comfortable.

The moment he stepped in, his first reaction was, 'Why is it feeling so chilly?' On being told the reason, Sachin simply opened the overhead windows and fixed the AC temperature at 35 degrees.

After half an hour of practice, he was dripping with sweat. Then, finally, he looked at me and said: 'I am going to Sri Lanka, and you guys want me to practice comfortably in 24 degrees!'

But the scariest recollection I have is of the 2010 IPL when he captained Mumbai Indians. In one of the knockout games, he split his right webbing while playing against Royal Challengers Bangalore. He had five stitches on his webbing and couldn't have played the final in the next three days. It was MI's first final, and he wasn't going to sit out. Not for his life.

He called up Mr Kohli of Vampire company, which used to supply him with gloves and asked him to use extra padding in the webbing area to protect the stitches as it was still very raw. As requested, the specially made-gloves were delivered to Sachin. He then went to the physio and asked for a painkilling injection to numb the area around the webbing. There won't be any sensation while even holding the bat till the effect of the injection was there.

Well, I was there at MI nets, and Master started batting. After some time, I was curious as the palm of his gloves looked unusually red. So I stopped the nets and went ahead to see what had happened. But, unfortunately, he was so focused on his batting that he didn't realise that the stitches had opened due to the impact of the ball hitting the bat, and blood oozed out.

Due to numbness, he didn't know that the entire palm of his gloves was now flaming red. He played that final with stitched webbing, and only a few people know about it to date.

Last but not least, I would certainly talk about his family, especially his wife Anjali's contribution. I have seen Sachin practice from 6.30 am till 2.30 pm with an hour's break and then fall asleep at the massage table due to tiredness. But when Sachin trained, neither Anjali, Sara, nor Arjun called on his cell phone.

They always gave him space in his pursuit of excellence and Anjali would only call someone else if it was urgent. But Sachin attended any calls only after he was through with his nets. The days spent closely watching Sachin get about his business was an education for all of us. As I said, I call myself privileged.

VIKRAM SATHAYE

When he stayed back for those 20 children

Sachin Tendulkar was what every mother wanted his son to be. The generation that grew up through the 1980s and 1990s. Sachin Tendulkar was a growth story of aspirational India, and I was fortunate to witness that amazing story in front of my eyes.

I was in Maharashtra U-19 probables when Sachin had already stamped his supremacy in international cricket. Well, I didn't pursue the sport. Instead, I moved into academics, completed my MBA, and started working at MTV.

In MBA classrooms, the 'New India' was about Sachin Tendulkar and his heady accomplishments in the post-liberalization world. Even though I was in a busy corporate job, I would also do a bit of stand-up comedy and mimicry of Sachin, Tony Greig and Ian Chappell. In my book '*How Sachin Destroyed My Life*,' I wrote about it. It was nine years back in 2014.

The imitation of Sachin got me a lot of recognition; since 2003, I have done thousands of shows. I always felt my journey was intertwined with that of Sachin. So when people saw me mimicking Sachin, I started getting gigs and did the 2003 World Cup with Sony Max. But the turning point was the 2004 Asia Cup, where I was invited by the Sri Lanka Cricket board.

I was supposed to do Sachin's mimicry at an event where India, Pakistan, Bangladesh and Sri Lanka teams would be present. Before that tournament, I had only met Sachin once; that was the briefest possible interaction for an MTV event. But when this Asia Cup function was supposed to be held, I was wary of whether he would take my act sportingly.

Sachin's friend and former India and Mumbai keeper Sameer Dighe came to my rescue. Sameer told me, 'Vikram, don't worry; I will send a message to Sachin. It will be fine if you just say "hi" to him.'

The show went well, and after that, Sachin came up and told me, 'Hey, I liked what you did up there.' It was like a surreal moment for me. Next thing I knew that I was having breakfast with him, Bhajji (Harbhajan Singh) and Yuvi (Yuvraj Singh) at the Taj Samudra Hotel. That is where I thought I had connected with him.

Generally, Sachin is an introverted man and a very private person. Those days, he was even quieter. But somehow, we connected and started chatting. In 2005, I started touring and chased Sachin and my friend Sunandan Lele. Thanks to Sunandan, my interactions with Sachin increased, and mimicry became my calling card. He enjoyed it so much that he would call his close friends and ask me to imitate him in front of them. He was very sporting. In fact, at his retirement farewell party, he told me to imitate him.

I will always be grateful to almighty that I got a chance to talk cricket with him during the last 10 years of his career when he played some of his best cricket across formats. He would call me in his hotel room, chat about his innings, explain his frame of mind, preparation with every minute detail.

In fact, at the start of our friendship, he didn't talk much about the game, but as he moved towards the end of his playing career, I could peek into his brilliant mind and understand the cricketer and the person in greater detail. We had a great group of friends, and we would hang out more often than not. He perhaps felt that having played age-group cricket, I could at least understand what he was talking about.

Beyond his cricket, the relationship with an ordinary, straightforward guy, who remained sane even after carrying a billion hopes, stays with me. When he told me to host his farewell evening at Waterstones Andheri, it was an absolute honour.

Now let me give you an example of the kind of human being Sachin is. There was an event in Delhi that Sachin attended, and I was also a part of that event. As it happens, an event with Sachin means hundreds inside the room, and it takes a split second for things to get chaotic. Everyone jostled for selfies and autographs, which was unmanageable at one point.

I had to say, 'IT is okay, Sachin, if you cannot oblige all of them.' He had already done 100 selfies, yet some 20-odd kids patiently waited at one corner and couldn't break human barricades in front of him. Sachin looked at me and said: 'Vikram, forget about anyone else. If I don't give autographs and selfies to those 20 kids, I will feel worse than them.'

These were his human qualities. Any lesser mortal would have gotten irritated with everyone wanting a piece of him. There's this cliche that people are lonely at the top, and your number of friends decreases when you are up there. But Sachin never had a paucity of friends. He had four or five groups of friends—one from his Shardashram, Shivaji Park days, Mumbai cricket, the Indian team, and Anjali's friends. Sachin is an example that you will only be lonely at the top if you choose to be lonely. It is okay, you may not share your life with people, but you can still make an honest effort to keep in touch.

One of our common binding threads is our love for music.

Sachin considers himself lucky that he shared a deep bond with Lata didi (Mangeshkar) and Asha tai (Bhosle). Lata Mangeshkar used to share her stories of recording some of her iconic songs. With Sachin, whether he is discussing

Lata didi or Kishore da, or explaining the modifications of his Ferrari or how to cook a mean Baingan ka Bharta, his ability for detail is astounding. I have seen Sachin describe the colour of his car for 30 minutes. There is nothing that he would leave to the surface.

Why he would make Baingan Ka Bharta in a certain way, he explained to me for 20 minutes. Sanjeev Kapoor won't explain with such meticulous detail. Sachin will listen and tell you if a particular song sung by Lata didi is composed by Shankar–Jaikishan, S.D. Burman, or Madan Mohan.

Anjali also loves her music; many of our evenings are musical. We have had evenings with Shankar Mahadevan, Harshdeep Kaur and Jasleen Royal. One evening, Sachin told me that we must invite Shreya Ghosal for our musical evening.

I was close friends with Shreya Ghosal and classical singer Kaushiki Chakraborty as an ardent music lover. We have a 'Bawras' music group, which also has Shantanu Moitra and Swanand Kirkire. Once, I told Shreya, and she said, 'Really, Sachin and Anjali want to meet me?'

Now that evening was one of the most precious ones of my life. Shreya started singing at 9 pm, and we packed up at 3 am. Sachin would ask Shreya, 'Can you sing Baiyaan naa dharoo?'

Shreya was like a jukebox and for six hours, it seemed as if she was in her house and just causally singing songs from *Amar Prem*, *Sadhna*, and *Pyaasa*, and in between Swanand and Shantanu would explain to us the nuances of those songs.

If you ask Sachin and Anjali, they would also rate it as one of their best evenings. After retirement, Sachin has started deconstructing his whole life and what has stayed with him, the music, his friends, and the relations. I really enjoy our conversations now, and he would recollect many anecdotes he had never shared earlier. And trust me, he has an elephant's memory. For example, he remembers the fourth ball of a 10-over spell he played in Antigua 25 years back.

He has scary memory, and I enjoy his insight on the game. He told me a story where he was watching an Ashes Test with his father-in-law Anand Mehta. That was the game where a Jofra Archer bouncer hit Steve Smith on the head, and the next ball, Marnus Labuschagne, came in as a concussion substitute.

And the first ball he faced, he was also hit flush on the helmet. The next ball that Labushcagne played hit the middle of his bat, and apparently, Sachin told his father-in-law, 'I think this guy will become a great player for Australia.' He explained why he thought so.

'When you get hurt, and after that, your feet are moving fine, it means you have a big heart as a batter.' His clinching line has since then stayed with me. 'Footwork is not in the feet; it is in the brain.'

I enjoy my friendship with him as his insights unfold new facets of life, and the conversations make you happy at the end of it all.

SAMAR PAL

I first saw Sachin in 1988 ahead of his Ranji Trophy debut match against Gujarat. I was a good friend of Dilip Vengsarkar, the captain of Bombay. Luckily, I was in the city that day, and Dilip called me and asked me to go and meet him at Bombay Gymkhana. He wanted to show me a little boy batting in the nets. So I reached Bombay Gymkhana grounds, curious and keen at the same time. How good was this boy? For the next hour, I was amazed to see this 15-year-old batting confidently at the nets.

After the practice got over, Dilip brought young Sachin to me. He was pretty shy then. Dilip told Sachin in front of me that he is your man if you need anything in Kolkata. He also told him to take down my number.

The Bombay selectors were a little circumspect about whether to play Sachin in the Ranji Trophy game against Gujarat. However, Dilip's persistence ultimately made the difference, and Sachin played that match, scoring a hundred on his first-class debut.

My relationship with Sachin started at the Bombay nets. Since then, whenever he came to Kolkata, he would call me. I used to go to the hotel where he stayed. The first time Sachin visited my house was in 1991. He was accompanied by Dilip, Lalchand Rajput and Chandrakant Pandit. That was the first time he had Chingri Malaikari (Prawn Malaikari). He liked it so much that he told my wife to cook and send it to him whenever he was in Kolkata. Since that day, whenever he visited the city, I would take Chingri Malaikari for him at the team hotel.

In 1996 there was a Day-Night game against Kenya at Eden Gardens. He called me on the morning of the match and told me he wanted to have Chingri Malaikari. He insisted on having it for lunch as the Indian team had to leave the following day. My wife was worried because she feared Sachin shouldn't have a stomach issue. After all, he will play a match a few hours after having prawns for lunch. He scored a hundred in that match. Later that night, he called me and said, "Dada, Chingri is my good luck." He also loved having mutton biriyani.

The other story I want to share shows a side of Sachin that has yet to be discussed. The Cricket Association of Bengal (CAB) used to organize the invitational P. Sen Trophy. Two big clubs of Kolkata—East Bengal and Mohun Bagan got top Indian players to play for them in the previous year. I asked Sachin if he could come and play for the Aryans club. He said he would not only play but would take an active part in team building. He got Ravi Shastri as the manager of the team. Big names like Rahul Dravid, Anil Kumble, Lalchand Rajput, Atul Bedade, Kiran More and Ajay Sharma agreed to play for the Aryans club at Sachin's request. We went to the final, but rain played spoilsport as the trophy had to be shared with Mohun Bagan.

Aryans club organized a felicitation ceremony for Sachin on his 20 years in international cricket. The function was organized at the Oberoi Grand Hotel. He had a match for India in Cuttack the previous day. He organized the flight tickets and arrived in Kolkata to attend the program. I was very touched and will remain forever grateful to him.

Sachin and I shared a great friendship, which is still the same. He invited my family to his marriage reception. I decided to stay at the Cricket Club of India. Sachin called me and asked why I was staying at CCI, as he had made arrangements for us to stay. He told me to send my wife and daughter to his place.

In 1999 when his father died during the cricket World Cup in England, he called me and gave me the sad news. He invited my family and me to the funeral. He was very emotional.

Our bonding has grown stronger over the years. Sachin, however, is still the same. He calls me, or I call him every month. Every time he comes to Kolkata, he gives me a call.

Sachin has visited my house on quite a few occasions. Once during summer, he came to our house for lunch.

Unfortunately, it was hot and humid that day. So he decided to have lunch sitting on the floor. I realized that day how he hasn't changed as a human being after achieving so much success in life.

He loves art. Once he called me and started enquiring about artist Jogen Chowdhury. He wanted to buy a Jogen Chowdhury painting for his new house. I met Jogen da and told him that Sachin wanted a painting by him. He immediately agreed. I got Jogen da to present his painting to Sachin during the felicitation ceremony we organized on his 20 years in international cricket. The painting is still there in his drawing room.

To my friend and someone I respect, I would like to wish Sachin good health on his 50th birthday.

BORIA MAJUMDAR

My first encounter with Sachin Tendulkar was at the age of 11. The year: 1987. As a child growing up with cricket, it was inevitable that I'd be mourning Sunil Gavaskar's leaving our cricketscape. Indian cricket, overnight, needed a saviour. Sure, Vengsarkar was in great form, Manjrekar had his sound technique, and Azharuddin had magic wrists. But truth be told, none of them was in the league of the just retired Gavaskar. It was then in a Mumbai newspaper that I read about Tendulkar. A child prodigy, he was being touted as the next big thing in Indian cricket.

Then came his debut series in Pakistan. It was terrifying to think how a boy of 16 would stand up to the likes of Imran Khan, Wasim Akram and the express debutant Waqar Younis. My worst fears came true when in the Sialkot Test, he was hit on the nose by a Waqar scorcher. Navjot Singh Sidhu, batting at the other end, recounted later: 'My immediate reaction was he has to be rushed to hospital. I was about to run to the other end when I saw Sachin raise his hand. In his squeaky voice, he said, '*Mein khelega*'. He had blood all over his face, but never once did he think of leaving the field.' These two simple words, '*Mein khelega*', best sum up Tendulkar, who has always worn his nationalism on his sleeve. Watching Sachin continue to bat and then cream a four off the second ball through cover, I realised we were finally seeing our saviour in action.

This realisation was firmed up when Tendulkar scored a match-saving hundred in England in 1990. In only his ninth Test match, he stood unbeaten on 119, an innings that successfully sent the cricket world a message—its next superstar was here.

But all these were trailers to the real movie: Australia, 1992. India reached Perth, down and out. The hallowed turf of the WACA, the Australian fortress, offered the bowlers pace and bounce and was where Australian gladiators tested the world's best. Only real men survived. Tendulkar, then 19, scripted a fantastic 114, a knock of incredible brilliance that made up for a tame Indian surrender. We finally had an answer to the Australian fast men: Tendulkar. His Perth hundred remains special to him, and we have talked about it many times.

By the mid-1990s, Sachin had become my hero, a singular icon we could trust with all our lives. The best, however, was yet to come. It came when a desert storm stalled India's run chase at Sharjah in a crunch game against Australia in the Coca-Cola Cup in April 1998, an innings Mahendra

Singh Dhoni considers his favourite. I remember the players lying on the ground with the storm blowing across the stadium. India's chances of making the final were remote. But Tendulkar wasn't done. Soon, an even fiercer storm hit the Australians. Not only did he propel India to the final, but as an absolutely stunned Tony Greig said, he was also going for victory in a manner only he could. He did achieve the elusive triumph for India on his birthday a couple of days later, with a century that gave the legendary Shane Warne nightmares about Sachin. Then, again, during Australia's Test tour of India in 1998–99, he destroyed Shane Warne.

But the 1999 World Cup brought to light his unrivalled commitment to the nation. Forced to return home after his father's demise, Tendulkar was back in action within days. His look up at the sky after completing that fantastic hundred against Kenya, a century he dedicated to his father, brought tears to the eyes of every Indian cricket fan. He had played out each word of what he used to say in an endorsement he did at the time, 'My name is Sachin Tendulkar, and I play for India.'

Cut to the miracle tour of 2001. While we love to talk of Laxman's 281 and Dravid's 180 at Kolkata, Tendulkar's five-over burst in the last session of play complemented the extraordinary Harbhajan Singh effort in bringing India victory. Of his three wickets, my favourite remains his dismissal of Warne with a googly Warne would have been proud of. Then, in the last Test of the series, Tendulkar hit a masterly 126, setting up one of India's best series victories of all time.

Some cynics continue to say Tendulkar is vulnerable in times of real pressure. Indian cricketers have hardly been under greater pressure than at Centurion in South Africa in the game against Pakistan in the 2003 World Cup. Kargil was still fresh in our memory, and the match epitomised what George Orwell called 'war minus the shooting'. Chasing Pakistan's respectable 273, Tendulkar was well and truly up against it. And in that one Shoaib Akhtar over, the second of India's innings, he stamped his mark on the game. That famous six off Akhtar over the thirdman has had entire TV programmes made on it. His 98 was an outpouring of Indian emotion, an innings of incomparable passion and intensity. Winning player of the tournament, Tendulkar was instrumental in leading India to its second ever World Cup final, a match that remains a sore memory for the legend.

How best to sum up what Tendulkar means to us all? For many like me growing up in an India that was falling prey to turmoil and secessionist movements, he was a ray of hope, helping craft a national imaginary that looked solid and resolute. He was a sign of India's resurgence, a quiet reassurance that things, if not alright yet, were certain to get better.

In the first Test played on Indian soil after the 26/11 attack, India needed to play well to get the country back to a sense of normalcy. The English set a mammoth 387 to chase. Following up on a Sehwag blitzkrieg, Sachin was unbeaten on 103 when India chased down the highest ever fourth innings total on Indian soil. Facing the cameras on his way back to the dressing room, Sachin took only a second to dedicate the knock to the victims of 26/11.

It needs to be put on record that Sachin is the only cricketer who, when he stepped out to bat in Sydney, Barbados, Lahore, Cape Town or even Lord's, got the same standing ovation. The pressure he has played under places his acts on the same pedestal as Jackie Robinson's breaking of the colour line in 1947 or Jesse Owens' defying Hitler in 1936.

I have often been asked where I'd place Tendulkar in the world sporting pantheon. My answer is: at the very top. For a country with a sporting record such as ours, he has given us a dream and has helped us turn it into reality day in and day out, year after year. It's time we go a step further and place Tendulkar on that unique pedestal that no Indian has ever aspired to, the one reserved for Owens, Robinson, Wilma Rudolph, Carl Lewis, Greg Louganis, Michael Phelps and Usain Bolt. He is India's contribution to the history of world sport, a man who gave us recognition on the pitch for 24 long years and continues to do so in anything he does.

He is Sachin Tendulkar, and he plays for India.

Hundred international hundreds. Impossible but true. A testimony to the greatness that can never be challenged by even the most ardent critic. Cricket has always celebrated

Jack Hobbs scoring 100 first-class hundreds. In most debates on the world's best opening batsman of all time, Hobbs has beaten his other illustrious successors like Sunil Gavaskar to the finish line on the strength of these hundreds in the first class game. They are a testament to his hunger and phenomenal run scoring ability. The difference between first class and test cricket is like chalk and cheese. It is akin to the difference between India playing Kenya and India playing Australia or South Africa regularly. Scoring 100 hundreds in international cricket is a feat that has once and for all set Tendulkar apart from his predecessors, contemporaries and perhaps also from a generation of future greats who haven't yet graced the field of play. He stands unrivalled; no cricketer has ever been or will ever be where he is.

How do we figure out the enormity of a batsman scoring 100 hundreds? How do we rate such an achievement? If there aren't any cricketing comparisons, how does this accomplishment stand compared to greatness achieved in other sports? Such comparisons, which are a fancy of every sports fan's imagination, help understand the feat's symbolism. The nearest comparisons are all from the field of athletics. Bob Beaman's 1968 long jump world record that stood for nearly four decades or, more recently, Usain Bolt's multiple world record breaking 100 m runs serve a good index. The first word to describe these is 'unbelievable'. Hundred hundreds is something similar. Babe Ruth's home runs, Mark Spitz's seven gold medal winning performance at Munich, subsequently bettered by Michael Phelps at Beijing, and Nadia Commaneci's perfect tens at Montreal are comparisons that help spice up the debate over the 100 hundreds. It is the pinnacle of achievement in sport, the very top which appears inconceivable to start with.

Now to throw in a few more yardsticks into the mix. The pressure of a billion plus fans every time he has walked into bat for over two decades, an ordinary team till the late 1990s forcing him to carry the batting burden almost alone and finally surviving at the height of his powers for a staggering 24 years with operations in his feet, ankle, hip, elbow and fingers. We are now talking about the Sachin Tendulkar phenomenon. No sporting great has overcome so many challenges. Wilma Rudolph beating polio on her way to three Olympic golds fades in comparison. So does the legend from Bowral, considered cricket's epitome of greatness. Bradman had never played with the pressure of a billion plus, never played a game where a loss was similar to a criminal conviction with a billion sitting in judgment. Bradman played a sport. Tendulkar played a passion and one that drives the world's most populous nation.

As we celebrate his 50th birthday and put together this tribute from men and women across the country and beyond, it is time to think beyond cricket. Sachin is bigger than five days of six hours on the field, lunch and tea, and 50 overs in a match indistinguishable from any other. He is a sportsman, an athlete, and he needs to be spoken of in terms of men and women who have performed feats in sports believed to be impossible. There is no need to compare him with other cricketers, even The Don. He has to be seen in the light of achievements thought to be impossible, which hardly has to do with cricket. Michael Schumacher, Diego Maradona, Dhyan Chand, Martina Navratilova, Michael Jordan, Sergey Bubka, Gary Kasparov? Cricket is just the game Sachin plays.

But how can someone love it so much? Sachin Tendulkar won't know the answer to that. He still doesn't. And we will spend our lives baffled. How could he?

World of Arts

LATA MANGESHKAR

Sachin calls me Ma, and I am delighted he does so. He is a gem of a person, and what I like about him the most is that he is soft-spoken, humble and dignified at all times. Never have I seen him raise his voice or lose his cool—and that is a great quality to have in a human being. My cricket-watching—I must confess I understand very little of the game—is largely guided by whether Sachin is playing. I often switch off the television when Sachin gets out. He is, for me, the embodiment of all that is good about the game of cricket and its spirit-discipline, morality and gentlemanliness.

In fact, when I watch television and watch Sachin bat, I keep clicking photos on my Ipad. I feel really good doing so. And later on, I keep flipping the photos and keep going back to some of his innings. You might feel this is childlike.

This conversation happened in 2013 ahead of Sachin's 40th birthday at Lata ji's house. A part of it was used in a special issue on Sachin at the time. However, no changes have been made to keep the flavour intact.

But then Sachin's batting converts all of us into children and gives us a kind of joy that few other things do.

In both professions, you need to be honest with yourself to make a mark. If you see Sachin, you will understand what I mean. His cricket is pure. There is never a shortcut to success, and he is the best example. He has always worked hard on his game and given it his best for India. When you are representing the country, you have a responsibility towards every citizen back home. You are playing for the flag and need to be an ambassador for the sport and the country. Sachin has done so with distinction all his life. He will indeed fail on occasions. Each one of us do. Every day will not be a good day. But as far as effort is concerned, there will never be an occasion when he hasn't given his 100 per cent. And that's what makes Sachin special. As an older person, every youngster in India who wants to play cricket should follow his example. Follow his work ethic and his discipline. You don't need the privilege to pursue your dreams. All you need is passion and commitment. You need to accept that hard work is your only option and never shy away from giving it your best whenever there is an opportunity. That's what he does, and that's why there is always a lot to learn from him.

Sachin has often told me he likes listening to my songs during tours and that they inspire him occasionally. He listens to them when he is travelling or when he is in his room alone, preparing himself mentally. I am absolutely delighted he feels that way. If my music can inspire him to achieve further greatness for India, I'd only feel privileged. We should all attempt to try and strengthen him in anyway we can. For he is doing what he is doing for us all.

I often feel Sachin was born to play sport. He has played cricket at the highest level with distinction for close to 24 years. I did not like it when he quit One-Day cricket. I still think he should have continued, for he has lots of cricket left in him. There's no doubt his passion for the game is undiminished, and he should continue to play Test cricket as long as he loves the game the way he does. In fact, even after he leaves cricket (and this is my opinion), he should continue to play the sport. He could start playing golf seriously, maybe some other sport, but I firmly believe he should play some sport as long as he lives. All his life, he hasn't done much else than play sport with complete commitment, so he shouldn't give up what he loves so much.

As a performer, it is greatly satisfying that I have given Sachin some joy with my music. I recall this recent event at the house of Nita Ambani, at which both of us were present at her invitation. We were meeting to celebrate Sachin's 100th international century, and I was asked to speak a few words on the occasion. Soon after I finished speaking, Sachin asked me to sing a couple of lines from the song 'Tu jahan jahan chalega, mera saaya saath hoga…' from the film *Mera Saya*, which he said was one of his all-time favourites. I did sing a few lines from the song for him and was happy to be able to do so.

I want to tell him that he should never lose his balance. Never move away from his core values. Always remember what made him Sachin Tendulkar, and never stop pursuing what he loves to do. He has a lot to offer to India and to his fans. And life has just begun for him. In fact, he is half my age! Happy birthday Sachin, and I will forever be proud of this son of mine!

ASHA BHOSLE

I have been watching cricket since 1956 onwards. In fact, I vividly remember watching Subhash Gupte bowl at the Eden Gardens in Calcutta, picking up a lot of wickets against the West Indies in 1958. I also remember enjoying Vijay Manjrekar and Polly Umrigar's batting for India in the 1950s and '60s. Growing up, I had a deep interest in cricket and enjoyed watching each of these legends in action.

Thereafter, I saw and enjoyed Vivian Richards for his sheer aggression in the game. If Richards was aggression personified, our very own Sunil Gavaskar was all class and elegance. And Sachin Tendulkar is a combination of both of these legends. He was equally good in attack and in holding on to his wicket, a rare quality in any batsman. He has dominated world cricket for over two decades and allowed us to speak of an Indian in the same breath as Sir Donald Bradman. To think that there could be an Indian who could be compared to Sir Don Bradman is in itself a testimony to how good Sachin was. As said to have the qualities of Sunil

Gavaskar and Vivian Richards meshed into one is like having the best of everything in one man. That's what Sachin was like.

I first heard about Sachin Tendulkar when he was 15. Raj Singh Dungarpur mentioned him to me and suggested that there was a Bombay kid who was special. Raj Singh was one of the most knowledgeable in cricket, and I always valued his opinion. If he said Sachin was special, then clearly, there was something extraordinary in the 15-year-old boy. Thereafter, my son-in-law kept raving about him and even told me about Sunil Gavaskar presenting this kid with a pair of his pads. Needless to say, I was curious to see him bat. Why was it that everyone was speaking about him? How good could he be that at such a young age, he had captured the imagination of many?

And when I did watch him play during his debut series in Pakistan in 1989 against the likes of Wasim Akram and Imran Khan, I realized that all that was said about him was justified. He was simply exceptional. A man who was simply too good. His batting is like Lata Mangeshkar's melodies, timeless and immortal. You can keep seeing the videos, yet you will want to see more. Just as you like listening to Lata Mangeshkar songs at any time of the day, you'd like to watch Sachin Tendulkar play for India wherever you are. That's why I call him cricket's supreme artiste. The best the sport has produced or perhaps will produce. And just like there is a Lata Mangeshkar song for every occasion, Sachin could adapt to all situations and deliver a masterclass. His ability was unrivalled in the 50-over format or in Test cricket. We could depend on him as Indians, and that's the best compliment one can give him. Your country needed you for 24 years, and you never let us down. Can there be anything better than this?

I am currently 90 years old. Yet I keep myself busy with my performances and my recordings. For me, there's retirement only in death. We have been born to work hard, and that's what I have always done. There is no substitute for hard work, which gives you maximum satisfaction. As performers, we create things, give people joy, and entertain. Sachin has done the same all his life. And his canvas was huge. He entertained a billion people each time he went out to bat. Each time he scored a hundred for India, the country celebrated together. He made us feel proud as Indians and allowed us to celebrate collectively. He was a kind of festival in himself. Only it would happen many times a year; he was that good! He should continue to give back to the game in any way possible for the rest of his life; that is all I will ask of him. Cricket is his arena, and there's no way he should ever leave his arena and walk away.

I'd fail in my duty if I didn't mention my personal gratitude to him. In this day and age, when achievers of his stature charge a hefty appearance fee for anything they do, he has never asked me for a single penny ever. He has come to inaugurate my albums on more than one occasion and has even modelled for my boutique but never has he charged a fee for doing so. Such generosity is unheard of in today's age. A sense of humility and modesty in him makes you like him even more. He has stayed grounded despite doing all that he has for India. And it's not easy. When you get such adulation, it is never easy to remain humble. Sachin did, and that's why he is special. In fact, whenever I have asked what I should give him to compensate for his time and efforts, he has laughed it off and suggested that I should give him something very personal of my own. Accordingly, I gave him the paper in which I had written out the song 'In aankhon ki masti' at the time of my recording. I had it framed and presented it to him, and he said he would put it up in his music room in his house in Mumbai. There couldn't be anything better than this, and I was delighted.

AMITABH BACHCHAN

'I haven't achieved half of what Sachin has.'
                    —**Amitabh Bachchan on Sachin Tendulkar**

Boria: What does Sachin mean to you as an Indian?

Amitabh Bachchan: He actually means India shining. He has made India proud on the world stage and has given the country a lot to speak about. Ours is a land with a 5,000-year-old history, tremendous heritage and culture; of course, ours is a land of incredible intellectual wealth. But Sachin has been able to add to this heritage and wealth. Every time there is cricket in the world, we talk of India and say so with respect and reverence. This has primarily been made possible by Sachin, who has excelled on the world stage and taken India to a position of pre-eminence because of his achievements over 24 years. When a performer does

---

This was recorded ahead of Sachin's 40th birthday. Each word stays true, and we find it very relevant to reproduce it here.

well despite adversity, he adds to the glory of his country. And that's what Sachin has done for well over two decades. He has made us all proud due to his feats of individual brilliance: and we, as proud Indians, have taken pride in these feats of Sachin.

Sachin stands for all that a mobile, progressive and dynamic India stands for—passion, dedication and excellence. I have the greatest respect for him as a performer and individual.

Boria: You finished the last answer mentioning Sachin, the individual. Can you please elaborate on Sachin, the man against Sachin the cricketer?

Amitabh Bachchan: As a person, Sachin is the exact opposite of Sachin, the cricketer. If, as a performer, he is dominant, aggressive and bold on the field, which are the hallmarks of a real champion, as an individual, he is humble, dignified and rooted. He has remembered his roots, making him an extraordinary person. He comes across as someone who has not let success transform him, which is incredible, considering the scale of his achievements. In fact, if you watch his expression when he walks back to the pavilion after he's out, whether a low score of after he is out for a century, you wouldn't be able to tell the difference. He continues to epitomize the values of gentlemanliness associated with the game of cricket, which we hardly see adhered to in cricket as it is played today. He can do so because his foundation (built on the values inculcated in him as an individual while growing up) is strong, and he has never wavered from following these principles and values.

Boria: As a performer who has been at the top of his profession for a long time, there is a distinct similarity between Sachin and yourself. What explains this professional longevity that the two of you share? How is it that the two of you have been able to be active for years and can keep motivating yourselves time and again?

Amitabh Bachchan: I am slightly embarrassed that you are comparing me with Sachin, for I don't think I have achieved even half of what he has. But, to answer your question, it is about a solid sense of self-belief, and it is also about being comfortable with the thought that you are not infallible and can make a mistake. Sachin knows that he is on a quest for perfection. It will always be. Every performance is. Yes, he will fail on occasion because even the best do. But the important thing is to retain the desire to keep learning and improve the next time you get an opportunity. That's what he has been able to do for over 24 years. Despite being the best in what he has done, Sachin knows he can fail and isn't invincible. No one is. At the same time, he knows he can learn from a mistake and improve. That's what he has done all his life, which explains his longevity.

Boria: What, according to you, will be Sachin's most enduring legacy at two levels, first, as a professional cricketer and second, as an Indian citizen?

Amitabh Bachchan: His legacy will be that he will forever be remembered as synonymous with excellence. He stands for excellence and the highest standards of it. Every Indian should aspire to get to where he has in his life. But, more importantly, he has sustained excellence for the longest time. That, as you well know, is a challenging task. But, there is little doubt that he will forever be remembered as one who did the country proud on the biggest stage of all and stands for all that is pristine in sport, ethics and gentlemanliness.

Boria: How is it that you both have never become predictable and have been able to offer us all something new through your careers?

Amitabh Bachchan: Again, you embarrass me, It is difficult for me to say what I have done, but Sachin, he has constantly been able to innovate and add to his repertoire over the years. For example, the cut over the slips or the slash over the point, which often goes for six, shots with a Sachin imprint. It is as if he invented them to answer the questions the bowlers posed to him. This is because he has constantly been working on his game, ironing out flaws and adding new skills to his already incredible range. He has challenged himself and raised the bar every time he has gone out to perform. As I said, his is a constant quest for excellence, which explains why he never turned predictable or sterile. I watched the game with bated breath when he batted and sometimes switched the television off when he got out.

And I am sure I am not the only one for the last 24 years. I'd like to wish him all the joys for his birthday, which is a milestone in itself!

FARHAN AKHTAR

Sachin and I are almost the same age, and he has been a part of me for decades. In fact, I am not alone in saying so, for he has been a part of billions of us in India. In fact, for one person to galvanise the country as he did is simply unthinkable. India is a huge country with many differences across regions. And to think that Sachin was able to bridge all these differences and could get us all together each time he was batting is no less than a fantasy film script. And yet it happened. Time and again. For months and years. That makes the Sachin story so very different for each of us.

When I was asked to do this piece, I immediately tried to think back to when I had first heard the name, Sachin Tendulkar. It was from people who were closely associated with the city's cricket circuit who would often come home and speak about this new prodigy. Each of them was highly impressed by this curly haired teenager and predicted a huge future for him. And each one of them was right.

When you are deeply invested in someone, he somehow

becomes a part of you. I used to watch Sachin each time he went out to bat; in the process, he became a part of my subconscious. Irrationally, I felt I could understand and say what he would do next while batting. And it once happened that a few of us friends were in a pub called Ghetto when he was batting in a match against Sri Lanka. Randomly I started predicting what I felt Sachin would do next. And you can call it a bizarre coincidence, but things started happening precisely as I predicted. So I would say he would hit a six, and he did. Thereafter I'd say he would nudge the ball around for two overs and score between 10 and 12 runs, and it would happen exactly the same way. In my mind, I was batting with him, and he was a part of me. In all this, the waiter who was serving us was the most stunned and terrified. He may have thought I was a bookie and seemed confused about what was happening.

My first Sachin autograph is again a story. A very close friend of mine used to cut his hair, and one time when she mentioned that she was going to his house to cut his hair, I sent three things with her to be autographed. One of them was a copy of the *Time* magazine, which featured him on the cover playing his favourite cover drive with the caption 'Burning Bright'. I still have the magazine, by the way. In fact, I mentioned it to him when I finally had a chance to meet him.

In a way, I have imbibed many things from Sachin, which have helped my career. The first thing is to stay true to the sport. With the kind of adulation and fame, he could have easily had a chip on his shoulder. He is Sachin Tendulkar, after all. But that's where he is different. For him, it was always about hard work and about trying to learn. He is always trying to get better at what he does. Staying a student of the game and keep on improving. I have tried to do so in my profession, and Sachin has been a constant source of inspiration. That's what he has been to me. A beacon of light which has unknowingly helped me along the way.

To tell you the truth, each time he got out, we felt unease as a collective nation. Our confidence dropped a little bit, and things weren't the same for a while. We needed him out there for us to feel well. Feel normal and happy. He wasn't batting for himself. Instead, he was batting for us all, for a collective called we lovingly call 'India'.

For many of us in India, the Sharjah desert storm innings against Australia in April 1998 helped shape the Sachin narrative. He was the lone man standing and was determined to carry India to the final. He wasn't willing to leave the field and, with singleminded determination, went about his business. It was extraordinary. That's what it was. A singleminded pursuit of excellence. Sachin pursued it all his life and, in doing so, made a difference in our lives. Touched us in ways, we never imagined anyone could. Shaped careers, inspired narratives and galvanised a country. Sachin nurtured dreams in ways few can, which is why he will always be very special. And yet, if you speak to him, you will notice his humility. He is still very Sachin and not the great Sachin Tendulkar. You can call him by his first name and not feel a sense of unease. He is one of us and will always be so. You can easily have a conversation with him and feel good about it. He will never make you feel overawed or small, and that's the beauty of the man.

To conclude, Sachin Tendulkar will forever be a part of me. We grew up together in Mumbai, and while we had never met, we were still very close. He was the absent present in my life who helped me all along, and I am ever grateful to him.

Wish him a very happy 50th birthday. Stay healthy, Sachin.

PRAHLAD KAKKAR

Humility made Sachin a larger-than-life brand

While discussing the brand Sachin Tendulkar, one thing that nobody should forget about is his humble background. Long before M.S. Dhoni came from Jharkhand, Sachin was the true representation of the Indian middle class from East Bandra.

Coach Ramakant Achrekar had two prodigies in Sachin and Vinod Kambli. Kambli was the obvious rockstar with his flamboyance and how he conducted himself. Sachin was quieter with a squeaky little voice. He didn't look like a Rockstar but he was the real rockstar. The best thing about Sachin is that his best friends were always Marathi-speaking people. Regardless of who he met later in life, he never lost those friends. So, here is a man who has always remained in touch with his mother tongue. That's his brand. His brand is his humility.

People only talk about his dominance on the cricket

pitch and accumulated runs. Nobody pays attention to the fact that it's not his runs but how he did it. He did it with great humility. He never behaved like a star. He behaved as if he was lucky to achieve the things he did. He is not one of those brands that scream and let you know he has achieved something. There are people who make gestures and statements when they achieve a milestone. Sachin Tendulkar quietly did it.

Sachin's resurgence in the early 90s was such that every woman wanted to adopt him as her son. Everyone prayed for him. Everyone wanted '*Kuchch bhi ho jaaye, issko bachake rakhna hain* ('Whatever happens, this kid needs to be protected')'. He became the champion of the middle class and remained the same throughout his journey. Every advertisement was written around this trait. The common man followed him.

Let me give you an example of his simplicity and being a middle-class man. Sachin and I stayed in the same building. His son Arjun was very fascinated by his expensive cars. He wanted to go for rides with Sachin. Sachin couldn't go out in the city all the time. So, Sachin would drive him around the complex very slowly until Arjun fell asleep. That's how devoted a father he is.

Sachin's brand value grew because he became an alternative to movie stars. He was a natural. What worked for him is that whatever he did in his life was not scripted. An actor's image is made through scripts.

To start with, it wasn't easy to work with him because

he was not an actor. But he was always willing to learn. Soon, I realized you shouldn't give him acting. He needed to be given objectives that he needed to be endorsed. I used to tell him to turn down certain things. 'You'll look stupid. The country doesn't need or can afford that,' I would say to him. I always told his manager and his close ones to show him down. Once he retired, he would eventually be bigger than anybody in the game. He will always be remembered for the great things; nobody will remember the ducks he scored. He is such a massive brand.

Brands should always look to endorse the idea of Sachin Tendulkar. Unfortunately, those who tried to endorse their brands through Sachin failed badly. Only Pepsi realized it.

Sachin's only condition going for ad shoots was that it should never come across that he was bigger than the game. We did a viral campaign for Pepsi called 'Sachin ala re'. In the ad, Sachin was supposed to dismiss balls thrown at him from the stadium with a fly swatter during a practice session. It was supposed to be released in English, Hindi and Marathi. He came and shot for it. He shot it just a couple of days before the ad was due to be released. He never interfered with what was shot but we still sent it to him for approval.

The next morning, he called me and said he was very upset. He told a fly-swatter in Hindi, and Marathi is called a '*makhkhimaar*'. The connotation of '*makhkhimaar*' in Hindi and Marathi is that a person is so big that everything is beneath him. 'This makes me look like Sheikh Chilli. I am no Sheikh

Sachin the big hitter

By SUNDER RAJAN

The Times of India News Service

PESHAWAR, Dec. 16.

SACHIN TENDULKAR today more or less set at rest reservation about his ability to adapt himself to the one-day game. He slammed an unbeaten 53 of just 18 balls as India lost an exhibition match against Pakistan here by four runs.

Tendulkar's blitz in the last overs of the match almost won the day for India. He began by nonchalantly lifting Mushtaque Ahmed for six over long on, followed it up with three successive sixes off the redoubtable Abdul Qadir and a four.

In all, Tendulkar hit five sixes and two fours to win the hearts of the spectators.

Chasing Pakistan's 157 for four, India finished with 153 for three in the 20-over game following the cancellation of the first international because of poor light.

Salim Malik, who contributed 75, was adjudged the man of the match.

The crowd waited patiently for Srikkanth, a popular figure here, but the Indian captain was pushed to the backseat by Sachin Tendulkar, who hit two huge sixes of Mushtaq. Tendulkar set the damp day alive by hitting three consecutive sixes of Qadir, a boundary and a three to produce 25 runs from that over before completing his 50 with a two off Akram.

Needing four runs of the last ball, India finished at 153. Tendulkar, remained not out on 53 and Srikkanth on 13.

Pakistan: Mansoor Akhtar c Maninder b Sharma 53, Saeed Anwar b Ankola 0, Salim Malik c Tendulkar b Ayub 75, Wasim Akram c Razdan b Srikant 4, Imran Khan not out 12, Salim Yusuf not out 3, Extras (lb-1, w-9) 10, Total (for 4 wkts., 20 overs) 157. **Fall of wickets:** 1-4, 2-134, 3-137, 4-140.

Bowling: Razdan 2-0-11-0; Ankola 2-1-3-1; Tendulkar 1-0-9-0; Maninder Singh 4-0-27-0; Arshad Ayub 4-0-41-1; Sharma 4-0-41-1; Srikkanth 3-0-24-1.

India: Lamba c Saeed Anwar b Waqar Yunus 26, W. V. Raman b Mushtaq Ahmed 42, Ajay Sharma c Saeed b Mushtaq Ahmed 14, K. Srikkanth not out 13, S. Tendulkar not out 53. Extras: 5. Total (for 3 wkts.) 153.

Fall of wkts: 1-64, 2-79, 3-88.

Bowling: Imran Khan 4-0-17-0. Wasim Akram 4-0-27-0; Aquib Javed 4-0-26-0 Waqar Yunus 2-0-14-1, Qadir 2-0-44-0, Mushtaq Ahmed 7-0-23-2.

The wall in Sachin's drawing room with the many awards and recognitions for all the hard work.

Sachin Tendulkar on debut in Pakistan 1989 when he made his mark with his sixes off Abdul Qadir.

Sachin has always encouraged sportsmen and sportswomen with disabilities and been a pillar of support. This picture is at the paraplegic rehabilitation center at Khadki, Pune. This center houses jawans who have been injured or paralysed in combat.

M.F. Hussain's gift to Sachin.

Walking back after one of many memorable moments in Australia with the opponents according him the privilege of leading players back to the change room.

With Mr Gavaskar, his idol, when he crossed the record of 34 Test hundreds.

Walking out to a 'Sachinnn Sachinn' chant. Only batter who received a standing ovation in all grounds of the world.

With his victorious teammates in Pakistan in 2004.

Explaining things to Arjun at the
Ealing Cricket Club.

With the revered Lata Mangeshkar who
always inspired Sachin.

Sachin has always had a
special place for the armed
forces and here he wears the
uniform with tremendous
pride.

Sachin's house in Yorkshire in 1992.

With Mark Mascarenhas—a friend and someone
who helped the making of Brand Sachin.

With Vinod Kambli during the famous
partnership of 664 runs.

Sachin always loved working
on his own bats. In fact, he
was the go-to man in the
team to get bats fixed!

A very special photograph—
with Mrs Anjali Tendulkar.

With the great Amitabh Bachchan.

With the legendary Asha Bhonsle.

The five who tormented world bowlers. With Rahul Dravid, Yuvraj Singh, Sourav Ganguly and Virender Sehwag.

With the Tiger.

In New Zealand when Sachin is trying hard to show
he isn't scared!

When the Master was born!

The gloves Sachin wore
while scoring his 100th
100 which he later on
signed and gifted to
Boria Majumdar.

Cake cutting to celebrate his 100th century!

Sachin Tendulkar at Eden Gardens.

Square drive against Australia at Mohali on way to surpassing Brian Lara's record.

Sachin in action for Mumbai.

Yet another milestone for the Master!

He gave it all for the country whenever he came out to bat.

Misti-mukh.

Chilli,' he told me. The ad would imply he is bigger than the game. He wanted to reshoot. He made a valid point.

I called the Pepsi guys, and they asked how it could be possible. I told them that Sachin had promised to shoot at any given time. We reshot the ad that day afternoon with a stump. And then, it went on to become one of the most popular ad visuals of Sachin Tendulkar.

To sum up, Sachin Tendulkar's humility made him the larger-than-life brand.

USHA UTHUP

How do I see Sachin? He is the greatest cricketer to have played the sport for India without trying to offend anyone who has played cricket with distinction. And for the longest time, he was an emotion for everyone in this country. We felt excitement and fear each time he stepped out to bat. We did not want him to get out, for that would mean India was in trouble. We would celebrate with him, dream with him and enjoy with him. He was the purest when it came to the sport. A true lover of cricket. And, naturally, we all will love a lover.

I had the pleasure of singing for Sachin on some occasions. I sang a song for him at a CCL function some years ago. And at the end, I requested him to come on stage. As always, he was humble and dignity personified. I think he enjoyed listening to the song and did say as much.

Many years back, we were part of a benefit match in Sharjah, yet again he was a true sport. I remember performing a song in Marathi, and Sachin joined in. Frankly, he did not have to. But he did so voluntarily and added a lot more to the occasion.

The best thing about Sachin is his humility. For anyone to be judged over a period of time, humility is the best marker. If you let your ego get the better of you, it will soon be all over for you. Despite achieving almost everything there is to achieve, Sachin always managed to stay humble. And that explains why he is one of India's most loved icons.

As the youngest Bharat Ratna ever at 41, he has set benchmarks. And in doing so, has inspired one and all. He is a story that each one of us is a part of. A true Indian tale. If he could score hundreds in Australia at the age of 19, we can also do things in our lives that seem impossible to start with. If he can wait for the World Cup for 22 years and go on to fulfil his dream, we can all face adversity and deal with challenges that come our way. If he can be recognised by the state and awarded the Bharat Ratna at 41, everyone who plays sport should feel inspired that each one of them has a chance. He is an aspirational story. A story in flesh and blood that we can all seek to emulate. He is real. A product of sheer hard work and talent combined. And he did not come from a privileged background. In fact, he is very much like each one of us. The boy next door who dared to dream and then went on to fulfil his dreams by working the hardest and staying committed to his dream.

As he turns 50, I wish him all the happiness in the years ahead and the best of health. Sachin Tendulkar is a national treasure that India will forever be proud of. Happy birthday and God bless.

Quotes from other artists

If Sachin Tendulkar is not a hero who is?

—Mark Knopfler in an interview
on 29 September 2017

Sachin is someone who has proved his worth through his work. The term 'My bat will do the talking' is the truest for Sachin. I have seen him in his ups and downs; I have heard people talk about him but he has always kept quiet and let his game do the talking.

—Shah Rukh Khan at the premiere of
Sachin: A Billion Dreams

Fourth Estate

LAXMAN SIVARAMAKRISHNAN

How Sachin 'swept' Warne off his feet!

When Sachin Tendulkar made his Test debut in 1989, he broke my record as the youngest Indian to do so. He was nearly a decade old in international cricket when Australia was to tour India in March 1998. Weeks before that series, I received a call from Sachin. He asked me to help him prepare against Shane Warne. I was thrilled that a player of his calibre thought of me to prepare him for such a vital assignment.

The entire series was built around the Tendulkar–Warne rivalry. They were the two poster boys of international cricket at the time. We decided to train at the MRF Pace Academy in Chennai.

Most think about the exact purpose of those training sessions. I was never going to be a replica of Shane Warne. But what worked for me was that I also had big leg breaks.

Sachin knew Warne would be looking to use the rough

created outside his leg stump by the likes of Glenn McGrath. So, we had to create rough and abrasive patches on the pitch. Sachin had bought new shoes with sharp spikes. He scratched the surface very hard and created the rough. The groundsman was not happy with what we were planning. We decided to use just one pitch for the week-long session. By the third or fourth day, the pitch became very tough to bat on.

Those were the days when you didn't really have video analysts and exposure to the wide range of videos like you do now. We spoke a lot. He gave me feedback from his experience of facing Warne. Sachin very vividly described the pace off the pitch Warne could generate. Also, he gave me a clear picture of the variation of pace, trajectory and angles Warne used. That's how observant Sachin was.

The most important thing when you talk about preparing for a series is clarity of mind. Sachin was very clear in his mind about what he wanted to develop during that camp. He wanted to grow a range of shots targeting anything from fine-leg to mid-wicket. So, he wanted the paddle sweep, the generic sweep and the slog sweep. Those days, there was just one sweep played by batters worldwide. It was the hard sweep towards the square leg. Sachin thought of the paddle sweep, which also cut out the risks.

He asked me to bowl a lot from round the wicket into the rough. Sweeping out of the rough is very difficult, so Sachin added the paddle sweep. Each net session was brief.

He would bat for an hour. It's not the quantity of practice but the quality that matters most. Sachin believed in that. Mind you, batting in the nets for one straight hour is not easy either and that too when you are playing aggressive shots. But his practice wasn't just limited to playing out of the rough. He also knew Warne's strength from over the wicket and attacking the stumps. He just wanted to nullify Warne's ploy to use the rough.

A week after we finished the training, Sachin played Australia in the first Test in Chennai. And he unleashed the entire range of sweeps to score a match-winning 155 not out in the second innings. That was the year Sachin absolutely ruled international cricket as a batter. In a week, he added a deadly weapon to his armoury. The sweeps, especially the paddle sweep, remained an essential part of his career.

JHULAN GOSWAMI

I grew up watching football. I still remember watching the 1990 football World Cup when I was very young; I was in class 3 or 4 and was addicted to the beautiful game. In fact, I used to watch only football and no other sport. Like most Kolkatans, I was a Maradona fan, and his exploits in the 1986 World Cup in Mexico meant we all worshipped him in Kolkata. I first watched a live cricket match during the 1992 cricket World Cup in Australia and New Zealand. It was also Sachin sir's first World Cup. It was then I started following him. He had already scored two hundreds in Australia and greatly influenced me to play cricket. There was a commercial with the catchline 'Eat Cricket, Drink Cricket and Sleep Cricket'. I started consuming Sachin sir exactly as the tagline suggested. Like many in my generation, I was just crazy about him without ever thinking that I would grow up to become a fast bowler. Those days people used to buy chewing gum, which had stickers of cricketers. I used to search for Sachin's photo and would only buy the

gum for the picture. It wouldn't be a lie to say I fell in love
with cricket because of Sachin sir.

It is strange to think that I only got an opportunity to
meet Sachin sir for the first time in 2007 after coming back
from an ICC awards function. The meeting took place in
the Taj Hotel in Delhi. After the BCCI had felicitated me
for winning the ICC award, there was a dinner party where
Sachin sir was present. I started shivering when I saw him
in front of me. It was strange. The reaction was entirely
spontaneous, and I was completely in awe. There were two
senior women cricketers with me. They, in fact, asked me
what happened? I could not talk to him (Sachin) properly.
How could I? Here was someone who was responsible for
me playing the sport I love so much. He was the one I had
always looked up to, and to see him in front of me in flesh
and blood was not something I could come to terms with. It
was a fan girl moment which had me tongue-tied. I did not
know how to react. In a moment of extreme excitement, it
is impossible to speak. And that's precisely what happened
to me.

I had watched him play all these years, but being
physically present in front of him was like a dream. For
days I watched him practice at the MIG club in Mumbai. But
I did not get an opportunity to talk to him. I still remember
his words that night. He told me the importance of diet
for a sportsperson. He also spoke about the importance of
training, especially for a fast bowler like me. What should

be the training process, and how can one strive to be injury free, to survive for a long time in international cricket. Very simple life lessons that had enormous significance for my career.

There are a few uncanny similarities in our respective careers. When Sachin sir was removed from captaincy by the selectors, he wasn't informed about it. An exact similar thing happened to me in my career as well. Nobody communicated the decision to me. When I first heard of the decision, I felt distraught. Thereafter I read in his autobiography what Sachin sir had said. 'You may take away my captaincy but can never take my cricket away from me.' I was very inspired by this comment. I was determined to never let the selectors drop me from the Indian team for as long as I played the sport. I am glad I was able to fulfil this promise.

Sachin sir came to our dressing room before the final of the 2017 World Cup at Lord's. After the final, the entire Indian women's team met him at BKC in Mumbai. Yes, other great cricketers motivated us ahead of this match, but Sachin sir was very different. He was like a deity, and his words had very different meaning. For me, his presence in our dressing room was the ultimate thing to happen. It meant we had done something special, and his praise still rings true in my ears.

While he has played some extraordinary innings right through his career, I have tried to judge him through the eyes of a fast bowler. And for me, his best innings was against Australia in the ICC Champions Trophy in Nairobi in 2000. How he played Glenn McGrath on that wicket, offering so much for the fast bowlers, was unbelievable. India went on to win the match. Another exceptional knock was in the final of the VB Series in Australia. In Test cricket, the one knock I enjoyed watching and can never forget was against Pakistan at the Chepauk in 1999. He was injured and was in extreme pain all through the innings. And yet he almost won us the match in extremely hot conditions. It was all about commitment and determination. A lesson in never giving up. For all of us who played the sport, it was an example of how a person can push himself amidst adversity. This innings of 136 spoke a lot about his mental strength and grit.

On the occasion of his 50th birthday, all I will say is thank you so much, sir, for motivating generations of cricketers. I have learnt discipline, determination and dedication watching you. You have been a role model and an idol for me. Not without reason do cricket fans call you the God of cricket. I wish you a very happy 50th birthday and pray you continue living for another fifty years. I also wish you all good health.

SUNANDAN LELE

When I saw his hands tremble while giving an autograph

Sachin Tendulkar is not God for me.
Because you can't emulate the almighty.

For me, Sachin is God's chosen one, whose humane qualities stood out as much as his cricketing magnificence.

I have known Sachin for nearly three decades, and I have seen a little sapling grow into a huge banyan tree under whose shade everyone found refuge.

If I have to recollect anecdotes of Sachin, even 10 volumes will be less, but for our readers, I will narrate a few, which would give us an idea of what kind of person he is.

It was nearly 15 years back, and there was a match in Mohali. I have forgotten the opposition, but I remember a call from a middle-aged lady, the widow of an Army Veteran whose younger son was suffering from a rare spinal cord-related ailment that had confined him to a wheelchair.

I vividly remember the name of the young boy. Fateh.

Now Fateh's mother called me and asked if I could arrange a small meeting of his son with Sachin as he is the only person the boy looks up to.

It's common to get such calls and impossible to always oblige to such requests, much to the disappointment of those who want that one moment with their hero.

But there was something in that lady's voice, a mother's desperate appeal, that I assured her I would fix a meeting with Sachin.

When I told about Fateh to Sachin, his first reaction was, 'Please invite him to the team hotel as at practice, there will be too many people and too much commotion. I might not be able to give him adequate time.'

So a day before the match, Fateh and his elder brother and mother waited at the hotel.

For some reason, the team meeting stretched a bit, and Sachin organised coffee for the guests and was apologetic for being late.

Finally, when he came, he was accompanied by a few players, but I will always remember what happened in the next 15 minutes. Fateh tried to open the belt strap of his wheelchair and tried to get up to shake hands with Sachin. His mother taught him to stand on his feet and greet elders.

But insane pain made it impossible for him to get up, and he sat there staring at Sachin. His eyes were transfixed, and there were two other Indian players, but his eyes didn't move.

It's still fresh in my memory when Fateh uttered those words, 'He gives me the inspiration to remain positive and fight it out.'

Sachin spoke to the family and posed for photographs and then was about to give an autograph when Fateh said something that stunned even Sachin.

Fateh looked at Sachin and asked: 'Can you put an autograph on my wheelchair strap that helps me sit properly. You and this belt strap are the two lifelines for me.'

I saw Sachin's hands tremble while giving that autograph, and one could see how emotional he had become. He knew what he meant to his countrymen, but this was unimaginable.

If that was the humane side of a brilliant man, I have seen Sachin the Ultimate Prankster.

Once, I was invited to a function in Nasik where Sachin was the Guest of Honour. When he knew I would be going, he called up and said: 'Sunandan come to Mumbai and don't go directly to Nasik from Pune.'

So I went to his place, and it was Sachin wanting to take his childhood buddy Atul Ranade and me for a spin on his brand new luxury car.

While driving down, I sat beside Sachin in the front seat for about half an hour before he stopped the car and said: 'Can you sit at the back and let Atul come in front?' I duly obliged, and we swapped seats.

After some time, Atul started feeling feverish. He was shivering, and Sachin stopped the car and tried to check his temperature.

'Yeah, it seems you are running a temperature. Okay, let's reach the place and will get you some medicines,' Sachin said.

He started driving again, but within 15 minutes, Atul looked like he would collapse.

'Master, I am not feeling well at all,' he said and watching him, I started getting worried as I thought we might need to take him to a doctor.

Sachin suddenly stopped the car and burst out laughing.

Now his friend was feeling unwell, and our man was in splits.

Then we realised that inside the luxury car, there was a temperature control gadget under each seat, and the driver could set it as per passengers' comfort.

So, Sachin's former manager Vinod Naidu and Sachin had our seats with the temperature set at 21 degrees Celsius.

But Sachin deliberately set Atul's temperature at 5 degrees.

A cold chill ran through Atul's bums, making him uncomfortable. Atul's face was there to be seen after realising that Sachin had taken his mickey out. We couldn't stop laughing for days.

Sachin's biggest achievement wasn't 100 hundreds but the ability to keep his counsel when a billion people wanted a heroic act every time.

So when I met him in his hotel room in South Africa after that 98 against Pakistan, he seemed so calm that it bothered me.

I asked him how he could remain calm when it was a billion, always expecting him to do the magic? Doesn't he get scared or fear failure?

He looked at me and gave an example.

'Suppose I am appearing for my board exams and I haven't studied the whole year. Obviously, I would seek divine intervention by going to every temple. Think what my parents would go through if I couldn't answer questions.

In my case, I study all around the year, so tough questions don't bother me any more. I am looking at opportunities and am not scared of calamity. I would be afraid if I am not prepared.'

Another incident that would remain etched in my memory would be my daughter's birthday on 21 September.

It was long back, and he had come to Pune for a charity event where he raised funds worth Rs 1.5 crore in 90 minutes.

After that event, he came to my house for dinner, and I had a picture of a birthday cake where Sachin was holding both my daughter's hands while cutting the cake.

I am a granddad, but that day I remember telling my daughters, 'Look, your dad gave you the most expensive present. Don't ask for anything more.'

I conclude this article by narrating one of my favourite Tendulkar stories. I carry a rice cooker on tour as I prefer to eat something other than hotel food daily.

I stayed at Taj Samudra in Colombo during that Sri Lanka tour of 2008. The team was in the same hotel. I called

Sachin and said if I cook would you come and join me for dinner.

He laughed: 'Tu Taj Samudra mein kahaan chicken banayega?'

I said you just come after the evening gym session.

I simply cooked daal and chicken curry and prepared a fruit salad. Then, we ordered rotis from the hotel.

Zak (Zaheer) and Sachin wolfed it in minutes, as it was after a gym session, and they were hungry.

Once dinner was over, we settled to watch Roger Federer win another US Open, but the TV was on mute as Sachin Tendulkar, an avid tennis fan, did a running commentary from the first game to the last.

Sachin's stories are endless, but I hope you like a few from my treasure chest.

SOUVIK NAHA

Tendulkar: a sleep full of sweet dreams

I came to know about Sachin Tendulkar in 1993 when I overheard my parents excitedly discussing his last-over heroics at the Hero Cup semifinal. In about a year or two, he was no longer India's next big batting hope but the person who stood between victory and defeat. Most of my friends in school idolized him as their favourite cricketer. I had other favourites. My earliest hero was Anil Kumble, then Sourav Ganguly, Rahul Dravid and Virender Sehwag for a decade. Early Tendulkar was like Tintin to me. Young, swashbuckling, high-achieving, terribly decent, honourable, inspiring, and insipid. Banal in conversations, predictable in personality, and without a remarkable literary character's usual depth and complexity.

Souvik Naha is an academic and teaches history at the University of Glasgow. His most recent book on cricket has been published by Cambridge University Press.

On top of that, Tendulkar commanded immense fandom—the nation swayed to his tune—and I thought the others needed my support. His consistent, almost mechanical brilliance was no less offensive than capitalism's dehumanized production chains. I swerved during the Commonwealth Bank series in 2007–08. After his match-winning knocks in the two finals against Australia, and afraid his retirement was around the corner, I yearned for the routine assurance to never cease. He now became my Gandalf. Timeless, warm, eager, simple, dignified, who commanded respect. Without a hint of pride, unconcerned with power, and hell-bent on making the team win, even at significant personal cost. He pulled India out of trouble so often that his rare failures were more apparent than his standard successes.

Tendulkar played match after match with broken fingers and toes. His injuries and tennis elbows—national tragedies—affected him the least. He never once lost his balance playing shots, fending deliveries, or carrying the team on his shoulders. Tendulkar made me feel good about my country like no one else. He still had the fire of the 90s. Tolkien described Gandalf's fire as a fire that kindled rather than devoured and wasted. An admiration for his self-effacing nature replaced my trouble with his linearity. This was a hero's narrative fit for a great cricketer.

The story took yet another turn after Tendulkar won India the World Cup in 2011. In the two years between the World Cup triumph and his retirement, he struggled against age, the laws of nature, and some good bowling. His returns during India's outings in England and Australia dented his batting average. As Poe created a space for death to gigantically look down on a marvellous city in ruins in 'The City in the Sea', Tendulkar's final days in cricket were a melancholic denouement. The team faltered with him, just as in the 1990s. I chose to deny the impermanence of his cricketing career. Keats had bonded himself to an old Grecian urn with an eternal interactive bridge. So did I with his cricket through books, videos and match reports.

The hundredth hundred proved as elusive as Hemingway's Santiago's 84-day wait for his prized marlin. The old man nearly destroyed himself in reclaiming his pride but refused to surrender to himself, his foe, and nature. He met every challenge with resolve. If the source of the old man's determination was his pride, Tendulkar's was his dedication to cricket and the nation. The hundredth hundred resulted in an Indian loss, and he drew criticism for slow batting. It was yet a grand transcendence of human limits—an unbelievable, inexhaustible cycle of self-regeneration. As his career drew closer to its conclusion, the full beauty of his craft emerged stronger than ever, for 'a thing of beauty' never passes into nothingness.

As Tendulkar got out in his final Test match in Mumbai, I quietly left the ground and took a train to Dadar. I walked around Shivaji Park, where it all began, before settling in for dinner at the Light of Bharat, where he gave his first interview. I set aside all my thoughts about his significance in terms of grand academic theories: false consciousness, charismatic authority, presentation of the self, society of the spectacle, celebrification, and so on. These theories have helped me understand why Tendulkar became a global hero, icon, and celebrity in the context of cricket and other social dynamics. But that afternoon, I just thanked him for the joy of watching him play.

I saw Tendulkar's fandom up close after India's match against South Africa in Southampton during the 2019 ICC Men's World Cup. A brigade of journalists and security guards escorted him out to the meadow next to the stadium, where he recorded match reviews for TV channels and gave some interviews. As he walked to the meadow, swarmed by cricket fans looking for photos and autographs, Virender Sehwag pointed to the crowd and shared a private joke with Harbhajan Singh, perhaps thanking Tendulkar for soaking up the public attention. Other legends of world cricket came out and got in on their cars uninterrupted. Five years after his retirement, the crowd followed Tendulkar as if the rest of the cricketing galaxy did not matter. He continued holding the country and perhaps even the world together.

VENKY MYSORE

I vividly recall my first meeting with the great Sachin Tendulkar in 1990. I was living and working in Washington DC, and on my bucket list was to watch a test match at Lord's. So I made a trip to London from Washington DC and got to watch India vs England test match at Lord's. Sachin had just made his debut in Pakistan in 1989, and one was already hearing about this superstar in the making. I knew W.V. Raman, who was also part of the Indian team, and he was kind enough to invite me to the warm-up nets on the morning of the Test match. That's when I got to meet young Sachin. There was something about him that one could see, and I requested for a photograph and he obliged! That continues to be one of my well-guarded and prized possessions! I have, of course, gotten to know Sachin much more since my involvement with KKR since 2011 and also on the golf course! His humility strikes you every time he takes time out to come and say hello and chat about cricket and golf. His genius on the cricket field has been well documented, but his down-to-earth nature and humility are always an example to emulate.

Sachin—I wish you the best as you reach an important milestone. We know your hunger for 100s and I have no doubt you will raise your bat again when you get that milestone. May god bless you in all ways, and may you remain a shining light.

ATREYO MUKHOPADHYAY

God of the nets, focus and dedication, unwavering

What to write about a person synonymous with centuries turning 50? Lots, lots, lots, and more have been written about him. Unlike some other all-time greats who preceded him, Sachin Tendulkar performed in the television and internet era. Almost all his exploits are there for the future generation to see, learn from and get inspired by.

Sachin is about my age. I was in Class X and watching on TV when he made his Test debut in Pakistan in 1989. Domestic cricket coverage on TV was not that commonplace those days, but finals and big matches were beamed live. I remember watching a 16-year-old, who had been widely written about since he was 14 or so, in an Irani Cup game where he scored an unbeaten century in the fourth innings in a losing cause. That was probably the first TV glimpse for Indians of what was to unfurl.

A mere sports reporter for about 26 years, during which

Sachin brought the world to a standstill and kept it in that state for 24 years, I must confess that I am not qualified to comment on his deeds, batting abilities, leg-spin, other turns and seam-up bowling or those flat arm bullet throws from the deep. He bowled left-arm orthodox at the nets at times, confusing onlookers who this left-armer was in a squad already with its share of it. There was this ODI in Nagpur in 2009 where a sharp, left-handed throw from mid-wicket resulted in a run out at the striker's end and ended the Australian chase. Ravindra Jadeja and Yuvraj Singh were the lefties in that XI. The former was bowling that over, and the latter was fielding at his customary position at the point. Who, then, was that? You know now.

Sachin is bizarre, a freak of the nature, ultra-talented, and we will soon run out of superlatives. We will still never be able to come close to describing to the fullest extent what we saw happen over that unusually long international career. In that case, the question is not what we saw but how did this happen? What caused this? This quest had been bugging me. I had been reading about him for a long time and had seen him play. I had noticed his intensity in practice during nets. I understood that this guy is also different because of the hours of intense labour he puts behind his art and craft, which is not seen by the public and fans. But still, I did not know what it took.

Before that farewell and 200th Test at Wankhede Stadium against the West Indies in 2013, I made it a point to speak to some of Sachin's Mumbai teammates. People who knew firsthand the answer to that question 'how'. Wasim Jaffer told me a tale. The Mumbai Ranji Trophy team was scheduled to have nets from about 9.30 am in the morning. Sachin had returned from New Zealand in the wee hours following an outing with the India team. And there he was at the Mumbai practice session, dot on time, doing everything others were. Jaffer said that the fraternity knew he was special. They used to go and watch him bat in club and other games before he had played for the senior Mumbai side. But Sachin's level of dedication that day at the Ranji nets was an eye-opener for him.

Pravin Amre, Amol Muzumdar, Sairaj Bahutule and Nilesh Kulkarni spoke glowingly about Sachin's commitment to practice. He hardly ever missed a session unless seriously compelled. And those days were few and far between. He could have taken it easy. Mind you, he was an international superstar already, well before turning 20. And what made him that? It was this heart and soul for honing the best of his enormous abilities to achieve greater heights, to enhance his gifted repertoire of skills. The names I mentioned were unanimous, that these tremendous and unbelievable levels of seriousness during training set him apart.

I apologise if I venture into territories I am not entitled to. I am nobody to comment on what I am trying to do here. But I saw Sachin at the nets, in India and abroad, from distant and close quarters. I was very close in Adelaide in

2008, nearly in a position where the wicketkeeper would be crouching against a spinner. I was taking photographs, and the camera was clicking with a bit of that noise. I thought this might disturb his concentration. Only to realise that he hardly had any knowledge of my presence. He had two things in his mind and sight. The bowler and the ball. Everything else in the universe was shut out when he was doing net practice.

Talent is something that every cricketer coming close to representing India has. What matters is, what do you have after that talent? What do you do with that talent? How do you optimise it? Sachin had talent very few possessed. The most talented ever would be an understatement. How did he transform that into an all conquering career which may never be matched by anybody else? The answer is his single-minded focus during practice. It's a pity that his nets videos are not that abundant on the internet. If one grabs some of those, the answer will become crystal clear. He played each ball at the nets from his heart. That's what made him what he was, the unparalleled.

RAJDEEP SARDESAI

I first encountered Sachin Tendulkar in the early 1980s when his elder brother Ajit brought him to a club match on Mumbai's maidans. The little boy with curly hair and rosy cheeks looked like he was just out of nursery school. He had an outsized bat and ball in hand and kept energetically moving around in the team tent. At tea time, someone volunteered to throw a few balls at him. Sure enough, he middled almost every throw-down and even hit one so hard that a few of us jumped for cover. Who was this kid striking a cricket ball even better than any of us aspiring junior cricketers? In the years that followed, we would get the answer: Sachin Ramesh Tendulkar, or 'Tendlya' as he would be affectionately called by his Mumbai mates, was born to play this game. Or maybe cricket was designed to celebrate his uncommon genius.

The writer is a senior journalist and author of *Democracy's XI: The Great Story of Indian Cricket.*

The inexorable rise of Sachin became a badge of pride for us Mumbai and Indian cricket romantics. It was almost as if we were all part of his incredible journey; we grew old with him, living, loving, laughing and yes, even occasionally crying in unabashed fandom. I distinctly recall a December day in 1988 when Sachin crept into my professional life. I had just joined *The Times of India* a few weeks earlier, attracted by the sights, smells and pleasures of a newspaper. A career in the Old Lady of Boribunder I knew would be challenging: the newspaper office, with its traditional hierarchies, was far too stodgy and slow-moving for a 23-year-old eager to make a mark. But, while I had given up on my cricket dreams, the maidan was still an intrinsic part of my life. So when I learnt that a 15-year-old 'aapla' (our) Sachin was to make his Ranji debut, I was caught up in all the buzz around the game. I reached out to my editor, Darryl D'Monte, a genial boss and requested an afternoon off to go and watch the game at the Wankhede stadium. Darryl had little interest in cricket: 'What's so special about a local match?' he asked. 'Sir, trust me, it's special simply because a certain Sachin Tendulkar is special,' was my enthusiastic response. Somewhat reluctantly, I was allowed to make the short trip to the Wankhede.

Fortunately, when I reached the stadium, a wicket had just fallen, and Sachin was striding out to bat. He was a boy among men, a teenager who probably should have been in class doing maths exams than facing a hard ball from 22 yards. But Sachin was made to bat, not wield a pen and pencil. Within the space of a few overs, it was apparent that we were witnessing a slice of cricket history in the making: the Gujarat bowling attack was average and just didn't have the skill to trouble a teenage prodigy. It was a smallish crowd—lots of Sachin's Shardashram school friends were in the stands—but the numbers somehow kept getting bigger as the word spread that Sachin was marching on to an almost inevitable century on debut. 'Shambhar' (Marathi for 100) was a word that Sachin had grown up with, probably a milestone he went to sleep dreaming about. Sure enough, Sachin got his 'shambhar' as he routinely scored right through his glittering career.

That evening I headed back elatedly to the office and went straight to Darryl's room. 'Sir, can I maybe write a feature report around Sachin for tomorrow's paper?' I asked. Darryl wasn't initially convinced: sports was meant for the back pages and was the exclusive preserve of the sports desk and not of an assistant editor hired to write on weightier matters of the state. Finally, after much persuasion, Darryl agreed to let me write an 800-word piece. The next morning, the newspaper's front page carried a headline: 'A star is born' with my byline. For the first time, I had got a front page byline courtesy of the genius of Sachin.

Life would take me through various personal and professional twists and turns in the years that followed. Still, there was one enduring, stabilizing presence: the sight of Sachin Tendulkar going out to bat for India was always comforting. From Mumbai to Manchester, from Chennai to Perth, every Sachin 'shambhar' was like a reassuring reminder of the little boy who never seemed to grow old, a Peter Pan-like figure who appeared as thrilled at scoring his first 100 as he was his last.

I distinctly remember how, after the Mumbai 26/11 attacks in 2008, being pushed into a slough of despondency. We had lost a school friend, a college mate and a few acquaintances to bestial terrorism. Weeks later, Sachin would score a quite splendid fourth innings century to take India to a memorable win over England. In that moment when Tendulkar raised his bat to the skies and adoring fans cheered him on, the agony of those bloodied days was at least partly erased by the joy of sport, a soothing balm to the soul. I remember smsing him with a brief 'thank you Sachin' message to acknowledge his contribution in lifting the gloom around us. He replied with a smiley, as he often would. However, high he climbed, his feet were anchored firmly on the ground. He would later describe it as the 'most meaningful' century of his record 100 international centuries.

For millions of cricket fans, Sachin at the crease meant all was well with the world, the iconic 'Sachin, Sachin' roar a collective expression of our passion for the sport and its ultimate folk hero. Which is also why when the 2013 India VS West Indies Test match was announced as the maestro's last game—quite astonishingly his 200th test—I made it a point to journey back to the Wankhede stadium. It was like going on a pilgrimage to pay homage to a deity who had touched all our lives with his wondrous skill set. As he left the ground one last time, I couldn't help but get teary-eyed. Our 'Tendlya' from the maidan was a global superstar, a champion drawing the curtain on his cricket career. I cried not because Sachin for once didn't get his customary 'shambhar'; the tears were not just of sadness but gratitude for someone who was a symbol of our unified hope and pride, 'aapla' (our) Sachin, who became India's Bharat Ratna, bringing more smiles to more faces than anyone else I can recall.

ANINDYA DUTTA

I shall never forget the day I first met Sachin. However, it is hard to forget for several reasons, not least being the fact that for the first (and only time in my life), I had a five-crore cheque taped to my chest.

No, it wasn't meant for Sachin, nor did it have anything to do with cricket. But due to a strange sequence of events that was to play out on the day, the five-crore cheque and Sachin Tendulkar would, in my mind, remain forever connected.

But I get ahead of my tale.

I arrived in the United States as a student with less than a hundred dollars in my pocket, dreams of a PhD, and an undying love for cricket. The latter, I was soon to realise, was a romance without a future.

Anindya Dutta is a banker, entrepreneur and writer with an undying love for the sport's history. His book *Wizards: The Story of Indian Spin Bowling* won India's Cricket Book of the Year in 2019.

In August 1989, Cricinfo had not been imagined; the Internet was in its infancy, Google was a decade away, and Indian newspapers rarely made it across the seas. Therefore, almost six months later, well into 1990, I first read in a back issue of *India Abroad*, a weekly newspaper published in the U.S., of a recent Test debutant, a 16-year sensation called Sachin Tendulkar.

Over the next four years, I treated my withdrawal symptoms from cricket with liberal doses of the NBA and NFL. If I ever turned to the back page of *India Abroad*, it was only to follow Sachin's flourishing career.

When I returned to India in 1993 to start my working career in Delhi, Sachin was on every billboard in Connaught Place. But my interest in cricket had waned to the point of disinterest. But, as the first light of 1994 dawned, that was about to change.

At 5 am on the 4th of January, I was waiting to board the first flight to Mumbai. Taped to my chest was an envelope with a cheque for five crores to be delivered to the Mumbai branch of the bank by 10 am. As a junior trainee at the bank, I was the courier trusted with this vital task.

Having handed over the cheque, I was told I was free to do as I pleased until my flight back to Delhi that evening. It didn't take me long to decide how I would spend the next few hours, for I had read on the flight about a Ranji Trophy match in progress at the Wankhede. Mumbai was playing Saurashtra. A short kaali-peeli ride later, I found myself seated at the famous North Stand.

It was the final day of the match and poised for an exciting finish. Much to my delight, Paras Mhambrey was sensational, scything through the Saurashtra lineup. I was thrilled not so much by Mhambrey's skill but his quick thoughtfulness paving the way for Mumbai to bat again.

Ravi Shastri, Sandeep Patil, and Sanjay Manjrekar had long been players I admired. But the man I had really come to watch was Sachin Tendulkar. His unbeaten innings of 80 that took Mumbai to victory alongside Shastri was sensational. The cover drives were sublime, pulls and hooks jaw-dropping, and square cuts a connoisseur's dream. Even his defence had me drooling. Finally, after three hours of watching Sachin wield his magic wand, cricket and I revived our romance. This time it would be for life.

Over the next decade and a half, as Sachin's bat wreaked havoc around the world, my encounters with him grew more frequent.

If our first encounter was in an unusual backdrop, the second was fated to end in unfortunate circumstances. Sitting with my new bride high up in the CAB Members stand, we watched Sachin score a magnificent 65 to get India off to a good start in the 1996 World Cup semi-final at the Eden Gardens.

And then it all fell apart. As India inexplicably collapsed, the crowd became restive and unruly. Finally, seeing alcohol bottles passed around by inebriated youth around us, we got up and left, just in time to avoid the violence and Vinod Kambli's tears, as it turned out.

Over the next decade and a half, like the rest of the nation, I was a slave to Sachin's genius. From the ecstasy of the Desert Storm to the declaration of heartbreak at Multan, the exhilarating upper cut off Shoaib Akhtar in the 2003 World Cup, to the disappointment of the final, I was there with him every step of the way.

His trademark first steps onto the ground with the bat in his left hand raised the endorphin levels by a billion. Then, his departure, with it under his arm, sent it plummeting. But through it all, Sachin remained his inscrutable self, being the best version of himself and bearing the cross of hope that never weighed heavy on his diminutive self.

As he waved from the broad shoulders of his teammates on a victory lap of the Wankhede after the 2011 World Cup, young Virat Kohli put the moment in context: 'He has carried the burden of the nation for 21 years. It was time we carried him.'

When I stepped into my fifth decade a few years ago, I celebrated by drinking in the genius of Michelangelo in every sculpture that still stands across Tuscany. A billion Indians will celebrate Sachin reaching that landmark somewhat differently, for he has been the genius that has sculpted their dreams.

I, in the meantime, shall be quietly raising a toast to the five-crore cheque that marked my first meeting with Sachin and reignited my love for cricket.

ASHISH KAUSHIK

Understanding his body like nobody!

I worked with Sachin Tendulkar for a few months leading to the 2011 World Cup in India. That was at the fag end of his career. He had already seen cricket evolve across generations. He actually lived it.

When I joined Team India, there was no overbearing aura about Sachin Tendulkar. His career has been such that he has seen so many different things about cricket and fitness. He was quick to reach out to us about anything he felt was necessary.

His body had endured a lot in the 22 years of cricket he had played by then. The best part about him was how receptive he was. Sachin Tendulkar was very particular about his rehab. He knew that was very important for him. He would trust us with the training routines that were given

---

Ashish Kaushik is the former Team India physio.

to him. He would never miss a training session. Sachin Tendulkar was very informed about what he was going through. It was always a two-way discussion with him. Based on his feedback, we would design training and rehab for him.

Let me narrate an incident when I was impressed by Sachin Tendulkar's knowledge. He once got hit in the shoulder while batting. Whilst everyone of us was brushing it aside as just a bone contusion (which is just a bruise and not a fracture), he was sure there was something wrong with the muscles in his shoulder joints. It wasn't that he wasn't in great distress or it was affecting his game much, but he explained to us in detail why he thought his shoulder muscles needed to be checked.

He talked to us about various injuries that he had. He explained the various interventions that were made on him during his playing career and also the experience of understanding his body based on the injuries. The way he explained it in detail, it was so convincing.

We explored various avenues and did several tests to examine it in detail. And as it turned out, Sachin was right about the shoulder joint muscles. We just had to give one injection to that shoulder muscle, and he recovered completely.

These days, everyone talks about workload management and injury management. Return-to-play is such a big issue. But with him, he always ensured that he had to be back restriction-free and pain-free. He would not rush. That's how well he understood his body, and that's one of the prime reasons behind his longevity. He always had a mature and informed outlook towards injury management.

He has had a long career, and he has suffered many injuries. His body's wear and tear can't be compared to many. But he never let that come to the surface. If you look at his fielding and running between the wickets till the end of his career, nobody could make out from the outset what his body had endured for 24 years.

DWARKANATH SANZGIRI

I first saw Sachin during his schooldays when I was invited by his coach Ramakant Achrekar sir. I used to watch matches at Shivaji Park and other grounds in Mumbai. He once told me, please watch one 14-year-old boy and tell me what you think of him. He called me thereafter for a match. It was the first time that I had watched Sachin bat. I was not an expert, but still, I felt there was something different in him because of how he played his shots. His intelligence, running between the wickets, placing the ball, and choosing the right ball to hit the right shot was all very different. Everything was beyond his age. He was showing maturity beyond his age, and the same opinion was given by several other Mumbai cricketers who watched him. Mumbaikars were keen to see this boy progress.

It was then decided by the Mumbai selectors that instead of blooding him in first-class cricket, he should be included as the twelfth man and should be allowed to experience the pressure of first-class cricket. So he was taken to Baroda as a twelfth man of the Mumbai Ranji team as a fourteen-year-old boy. So I also went to Baroda for that match.

Next year he was given the first opportunity to play in the Ranji Trophy. It was a match against Gujarat in Bombay (11 December 1988). I was lucky to be seated next to Vasu Paranjpe in the press box. We wrote the entire scoresheet of Sachin's innings, ball by ball, and what he did in that innings. He scored a hundred on his debut as a fifteen-year-old boy.

During this time, I became very good friends with his brother Ajit. Ajit wanted to write for *Sakal* and had come to meet me. Since then, we became good friends.

After his first season, everybody thought he would be picked for the tour to the West Indies. But the selectors were apprehensive that he could get hit by the Caribbean pacers, who were the fastest bowlers at that time. They felt that in case of such an accident, he would lose confidence early on in his career. I still remember Vasu Paranjpe telling Raj Singh Dungarpur, 'Arre woh lagne wala batsman nahin hain, who lagane wala batsman hain ('He is not someone to get hit but one who will hit the bowlers.').' Then I interviewed him for the first time at his aunty's place. Ajit had taken me. I asked him whether he would have loved to go to the West Indies. He was not very talkative then. Words never flowed like his strokes in those days. He said he would have loved to go and play in the Caribbean, and I could see the confidence in his eyes.

During the next tour to England in 1990, India had a tour

match against Derbyshire. Madhav Mantri was the manager of the India team. Young Sachin approached Madhav Mantri and said that he wanted to play and bat higher up at No. 3. He told Madhav Mantri he wanted to face Ian Bishop. Sachin was very keen to face fast bowling. He was very shy at that time but looked very confident. Before travelling to England, Sachin came to my house with Ajit. I still remember the day as he was to fly to England the next day. They had come for breakfast. We had sheera (halwa) puri, and medu vadas. After breakfast, I went out to find a taxi for them because, at the time, he did not have a car. Before leaving our house, my wife gave prasad and he carried it with him. He followed this ritual on many more tours.

After this series, he had grown in stature each time he came to my house. Till he retired, he came to my house once every year. Those are my cherished memories.

Whenever he knew I was ill, he would inquire and visit. In 2004 during a tour to England, I had to be hospitalized and return to India. In England, I used to live with a friend of mine. Sachin managed to get his number and called me. By that time, however, I had come back to India.

When I was about to have my angioplasty, I was on the stretcher about to be taken to the operation theatre. Sachin called the doctor (managed to get his number) who was treating me and ensured everything went off well. It was a great solace to me in that hour of anxiety.

I am not keeping well at the moment, and it was nice to

see him and Ajit a few days earlier. They had come to check on me. He called me the day before and asked if he could come and visit me. He was here for almost three hours, and we discussed cricket and other things. Then when he went out, there was a large crowd in front of my house, which proved how popular he still is.

Sachin's human qualities are tremendous. Let me narrate one incident which I can never forget. We had a program in the O2 hall in England. After the program, he had to attend a party. I told him and Sunny (Sunil Gavaskar) to rush out after the show because there was a large gathering, and he had to attend the party. If they waited any longer, he would get delayed. After the show, he noticed a boy with crutches in one hand and an autograph book in the other near the stage. He stopped momentarily, gave an autograph, and took a photo. After that, he had to sign hundreds of autographs and got late for his next engagement. But he did not mind. To him, bringing smiles to people's faces matters the most.

I have seen many great cricketers in my life right from the 1970s to date, but Tendulkar is someone special. His popularity sets him apart from the rest. Whenever he scored a hundred, there was joy on the faces of people across India as they considered him to be a part of their family. That is what Tendulkar is all about. He was lucky that he came into prominence when Manmohan Singh was the finance minister. Manmohan Singh changed the Indian economy from socialism to a free market, taking Tendulkar to almost every household in India.

I have not seen anyone's birthday being celebrated like it is for Sachin. People eagerly wait for 24 April to celebrate Sachin Tendulkar's birthday. Now he is completing fifty years, which is a milestone. But for Sachin Tendulkar, fifty was never a milestone. His milestone was always a hundred. He was always known as a century-maker. He has completed hundred 100s in international cricket and I am sure he will add one more hundred to it, the hundred of his life. I may not be alive then, but I will be clapping for this hundred wherever I will be.

ARANI BASU

Sachin Tendulkar had become a household name even before I turned 10. He was already an emotion in the mid-90s. When cable television began invading homes during the 1996 World Cup in India, Sachin Tendulkar's Peter Parker-to-Spiderman-like transformation was complete, captivating almost every Indian. Yes, the lovable, polite boy next door had turned into a superhero under the new jazzy floodlights in stadiums across India that March.

The Sachin Tendulkar fever was now a mania. Every local bat-seller would have his photo on the blade or the sponsor sticker he used on his bat.

I came from an industrial town in Asansol, which is 200 kilometres from Kolkata. But, such was Tendulkar's impact that the 'paid channel' exploded even before we could get used to cable TV. 'Paid channel' meant many of India's matches on tour were not played out at home. So, electronics stores became the hub when India toured England a couple of months after the 1996 World Cup.

The evenings turned into eerie nights very quickly in such a small town. Yet, the electronics stores would be buzzing. People thronged the stores to just get a glimpse of Tendulkar batting in England. They would disperse as soon as he was dismissed, and the store would seem like an abandoned *haveli* in a remote village. Sourav Ganguly's emergence on that tour did intrigue the Bengali crowd, but Tendulkar's pull was unworldly. He was a global brand that was driving India's post-liberalization identity. He was the face of a booming India.

The euphoria around Tendulkar was such that cricket academies started mushrooming in that industrial belt which was primarily dominated by academics and highly qualified engineers from the best institutes across the country. Sachin Tendulkar was a textbook in himself. The punch straight drive became a style statement of sorts. It's just that it barely came off for us. Coaches would tell me the days one drives straight with minimum fuss; one should know that batter is in peak form. But, again, it barely happened. Soon, one realized that Tendulkar's straight drive has an aspirational value, like the finest piece of jewellery.

I had heard stories of people turning off their television sets when Tendulkar would get out. I personally despised such behaviour. After all, 11 players play for a team. That's the first thing taught by coaches in a team sport. Then the famous 2002 Natwest final happened at Lord's. Tendulkar walked back at 146/5; I turned off my TV set and went to sleep. After that, the Tendulkar obsession happened very quietly.

That no individual is above the team is best demonstrated by Tendulkar himself. He thrived while opening the batting in ODIs then. Yet, he batted down the order so that India could maximize the ferocity of Virender Sehwag. India may have had benefitted from that in 2002, but it backfired in the 2007 World Cup.

Amidst all the hysteria, his silence during the match-fixing scandal in 2000 has often been questioned. But very few realized he was perhaps the biggest reason the wise people kept coming back to watch cricket post that episode that triggered a general sense of mistrust and literal disgust for Indian cricket. For a brief moment, the people of India may have ditched cricket, but they just couldn't part from Tendulkar. Again, this comes from the experience of observing an intellectual community in that industrial belt. That, for me, is Sachin Tendulkar's biggest contribution in dealing with the ugliest period of Indian cricket.

I was just starting out as a sports journalist for *The Times of India* when Sachin Tendulkar made amends for that horrific 2007 World Cup guiding India to the 2011 World Cup title. The desk worked overtime to keep the special pages ready to celebrate his impending 100th hundred. I knew the assignment to cover Sachin Tendulkar would not come easily to me. But that one year when everyone waited and prayed for him to breach the 100-century mark taught me much about how to respect a career. It has become a benchmark since.

As I went through the grind in journalism, the impact of Sachin Tendulkar on Indian cricket's Gen Z became all the more evident. Every second cricketer playing U-19s would name Sachin Tendulkar as his role model. Unmukt Chand, India's U-19 World Cup-winning captain in 2012, would never be tired of mentioning Sachin Tendulkar's unworldly twin centuries against Australia in Sharjah in 1998.

'What inspired you to become a cricketer?' was my rhetorical question.

'I was five years old then. I vaguely remember how Sachin went berserk that night. He was a big inspiration for me. I tried to watch him bat as much as I could after school and used to switch off the TV after he was dismissed and got on with my other work,' Unmukt had told me.

The Indian cricket board (BCCI), across regimes, understood the impact Tendulkar could have on the next generation. When I got to know Unmukt's U-19 India team had a session with Tendulkar before departing for the U-19 World Cup, I couldn't help but probe him about what was said in the session.

'The highlight of the session was his talk on dealing with pressure. He made us aware of the pressure of playing in a live telecasted event. Very few of us had played in front of the camera prior to that. He said the best way to handle the pressure of a big tournament is by stopping thinking about it off the field. He told us to hang out often and stay together all the time. He told all of us we could only perform like a team if we believed we were one off the field as well,' Unmukt had revealed. It just amazed me how Tendulkar could put his finger on the minutest of detail.

I covered Sachin Tendulkar live for the first time when he turned up for Mumbai to play a rain-affected Ranji Trophy semi-final against Services at the Air Force Ground in Palam. The aura of Sachin Tendulkar could be felt at such a tiny facility when you saw nobody dared to go into the small room where he would work on his bat. But that doesn't really help in understanding the personality.

So, learning from youngsters about their interactions with him became a habit for me. To name Tendulkar as their inspiration was kind of a template for cricketers born before 2000. Rishabh Pant took a lot of time to get over the fact that Sachin Tendulkar had asked for his bat after he scored a mind-boggling triple-century in a Ranji Trophy match against Maharashtra in Mumbai. He was 19 at the time. Tendulkar signed it, wishing him luck on the back of the bat. Pant has not played with that bat since. It's safely lodged in a case in his home.

I pushed my luck during an interview with Shubman Gill. By the time Gill played in the U-19 World Cup, Virat Kohli had become the undisputed poster boy of Indian cricket. 'I don't remember much, but I do recall the straight drive Sachin sir used to play. I was fascinated by it,' Shubman told me while talking about the earliest impression of cricket. The conversation happened just before he was named in India's Test squad for the first time in 2019.

The conversation with Shubman took me back to the last match, where I covered Sachin Tendulkar. It was the last Test against Australia at Ferozeshah Kotla, where India completed a 4–0 rout in March 2013. As India inched closer to the target in the fourth innings, the crowd celebrated Murali Vijay's wicket because it enhanced the chance of Tendulkar coming out to bat. A young Virat Kohli was visibly upset. It was still not known if it was going to be Sachin Tendulkar's last innings on Indian soil.

Once the match was over, the media asked the then India captain M.S. Dhoni if the world had seen the last of Sachin Tendulkar play. 'Be careful of speculation. Never rule out Sachin Tendulkar,' Dhoni had said with a smirk. That statement still holds true!

KUSHAN SARKAR

Life is 'Sach', and 'Sach' is Life

Let's not waste our time eulogising Sachin Tendulkar.

He doesn't need it from me. I am not important to him.

But yes, he is extremely important to me, for those massive moments and the accompanying little joys of life, for being an eternal hope that makes life so livable.

Since this book allows me that indulgence to put into words what I feel about the man, I couldn't have let this chance go.

I vividly remember before the tour of 1989, when the Indian team was leaving for Pakistan, the Doordarshan in its 9 pm news carried the airport departure shots, and you first got a passing glimpse of a man who ruled my life for the next two-and-a-half decades. And does so even now.

He entered my life through those grainy pictures of a black and white Telerama, and little did I know that he would remain equally relevant, if not more, when streaming and other social media platforms would have seized our airtime.

Sachin Tendulkar is a lot of things for me. Memories of my late father, who would grudgingly allow me to sit in front of the TV set for those extra minutes before exams.

For that, one more cover drive that would lessen the pain and scars that thermodynamics would cause.

For standing in the queue for three hours to buy a couple of tickets for a double wicket tourney at the Salt Lake Stadium where he was supposed to play alongside Vinod Kambli.

As Sachin crossed the athletics track to station himself at the boundary, my frail father, otherwise an introverted man, would do the unimaginable.

A big bodied six foot plus gentleman was right next to us, and once the star was near the boundary ropes, everyone stood up and 11-year-old me had no chance of catching a glimpse.

My father requested the big man if he could lift me on his shoulders for some time as I needed to at least get a glimpse of Sachin.

I don't know who that kind Uncle was, but he lifted me on his shoulders for a good five minutes before my embarrassed dad asked me that its time to get down.

The Pepsi campaign 'Yeh Dil Mange More' was yet to be coined in 1991, but you always knew what it meant.

Sachin was a reason for affection but Sachin also became the reason for his anger.

The 1993 Hero Cup was one such occasion. It was held just after our Puja vacations, and the semi-final against South Africa fell a week after the school had reopened.

I remember convincing my father that there was no Unit Test on that particular day, and we had this whole group from our locality who were going for the match. I had paid from the meagre pocket money that I got during the festivities and paid a princely sum of 120 bucks for a ticket. He was angry, but he let me go.

That first floodlit match under Eden lights and that last over to Brian McMillan is still so fresh in my memory.

From the upper tier of the High Court End, the memory of an ecstatic Vijay Yadav running towards Sachin after the last ball was bowled remains a forever memory.

Those were pre-beefed up security days but 90,000 lighting up the paper torch was a spectacle.

I was present at the India versus Pakistan T20 World Cup game at the MCG, and the gleaming Android torch lights were quite a scene, but perhaps in my 40s, the mind jogs back to hold hands with an impressionable 13-year-old who was amazed at the scene after that last over from the Master.

But a few weeks later, the last over did come to haunt me as my father attended a PTM (New lingo for good old Parents-Teachers Meeting) and came to know that there were two class Tests—English and Geography, that I had skipped, lied to him just to watch Sachin live.

My father did pack a punch in that slap that landed hard on my right cheek.

I lied. All for you, Sachin.

We often hear that 'Where were you when Sachin hit…?'

It was never about where I was when Sachin hit those two Desert Storm hundreds or that unbelievable hundred at Durban before that or when Shoaib Akhtar was sent packing over the thirdman fence.

It was always about what I would have done had Sachin not played those knocks?

What would I have possibly done if Sachin had not scored a double hundred against New Zealand at Ahmedabad in 1999, just weeks after my father passed away?

I was in mourning, but at least for one day in that month of October, I could deflect my pain of losing my dad for some time. Watching Sachin bat was always cathartic. He helped me heal.

What would I have done if Sachin didn't score that magnificent hundred during that historic 2001 series on a tricky Chennai track against Australia when I had just suffered a heartbreak?

That was grit and beauty at the same time. I didn't realise it then, but perhaps, each of his strokes during that innings helped me move on.

What would I have done if 98 at Centurion hadn't happened?

I was a 23-year-old unemployed youth with an uncertain future. Yet, by the end of that knock, I felt rejuvenated after feeling down for months. A permanent journalism job had to wait another nine months, but I didn't stop trying.

Sachin never tried to become a life coach, but he did become one.

The angry, disillusioned me in my new job learnt a lot about waiting and trying to quietly bide time when the chips are down.

How did I learn about it? From that Dale Steyn spell that Sachin saw off in Durban during the business end of his career.

Rabindranath Tagore had a song for every season and every reason.

Sachin Tendulkar had an innings for every season and for every reason.

I was fortunate that I got a chance to cover his farewell Test in Mumbai.

A day before the match, Sachin obliged everyone with group photographs, and there was one with all the covering journalists.

I still can't figure out why, but I stood a few meters away as I saw my super seniors, seniors, contemporaries and a few juniors jostling for space around the maestro.

But what struck me was his utmost humility as he said that on the chairs on his both sides, he would want all those scribes to sit who had covered his first series in Pakistan in 1989.

I missed a chance to have a photograph with Sachin. There's a slight regret as I have had the privilege of doing multiple interviews with him, thanks to his wonderfully efficient team, but I could never bring myself to tell him how I felt.

My mother was hospitalised in 2021 for a complication when Covid was at its peak. Like everyone else, we were tense and worried due to her co-morbidities.

I remember interviewing Sachin once during that phase, and half an hour after the call was over, I saw a 'private number' flash on my screen. It was Sachin Tendulkar enquiring about my mother's health, and I was at a loss for words.

My dear friend Bhavisha, who works closely with Sachin, knew about my mother's health and had intimated him. Of course, he didn't need to but his call touched me. In those tense days, it did help me keep my counsel.

I have never forgotten what Harbhajan Singh once told me about Sachin.

'Woh jeetna audhe mein baade bante gayein, woh aur zyada logon se jhuk kar baat karna seekhe. Yehi humility ak insaan kaisa hai woh darshata hai ('The more Sachin grew in stature, the more humble he became while interacting with people. That humility gives you an idea of what kind of human he is.').'

We are, at best, stargazers, but can I ask more from life than I came in touch with an artist, a genius.

Shouldn't I be counting my blessings?

Thank You, Sachin, for everything.

GIDEON HAIGH

Sachin Tendulkar 50?

For all that we heard it 264 times in international cricket, it arrives with a jolt. In our mind's eye, players tend to remain fixed, unchanged and unchanging.

Tendulkar had a certain immutable quality, regularity reinforced by his role: 84 per cent of his Test innings began at the fall of the second wicket, at which he emerged unfailingly as a cuckoo in a clock announcing the hour. Not for him, the modern cricketer's endless prating about the role ('Everyone knows what their role is'; 'I've discussed my role with the coach/captain/selectors'). Tendulkar grasped his role instantly: his role was to be great.

Still, 50 is 50. And Tendulkar was so young for so long. I first saw him, aged 17, in the Lord's Test of 1990—too young to vote, to shave, and tiny, a sporting cherub more closely resembling a jockey than a cricketer. Under that helmet, though, a hard head, as I came to understand at Old

Trafford, where his century righted a listing team after his elders had failed. Part of him remained that cool-headed, warm-blooded boy too. To the end of his career, he retained a youthful passion for the game, blending into every training session as though it were his first. You studied him for signs of boredom, of fatigue, of satiety.

Nope, nada, nothing doing. Had it been possible, you felt, Tendulkar would have played forever; as it was, it only seemed like he did.

50 then—which means that a good many years have passed since the feats that built his stature.

The elapse of time has historicised those feats also. Of course, Tendulkar was half as old when he propelled India to victory in the 1998 Coca-Cola Cup with 134 from 131 balls in Sharjah, having helped them qualify for the final with 143 off 131 balls two days earlier. He had been 18 during 1992's Perth Test when he plucked 114 from India's wrecked first innings; Sachin would be 30 when he dropped anchor in 2004's Sydney Test, famously abjuring the cover drive for 10 hours as he accumulated an unbeaten 241.

Tendulkar's 150s in the 2007–08 Border–Gavaskar Trophy came when he was 34, and whole generations had moved on since his debut, but he had not. Even then, the Indian Premier League was appearing on the horizon, over which he pronounced a kind of benediction by playing in the half dozen seasons, even if the format always seemed a little small for him, like trying to compress *Mughal-E-Azam* into a half hour with advertisements or the Mahabaratha into a haiku.

Think of what most of us are doing at those ages. Usually, we are getting started on lives and careers. At best, we are collecting the building blocks of success, which we might then hope to pile. Tendulkar was levelling the site, laying the foundations, erecting the walls, tiling the roof, then doing it again next door, next door, and next door, until he had laid out a vast, carefully planned city of runs. Sometimes we talk of the tendency of Test matches in India to suddenly accelerate—to 'go into fast-forward'. Thanks to his early precocity, rapid maturity, extended eminence and reinvention capacity, Tendulkar lived his cricket decades at a headlong pace, gathering momentum that has continued carrying him forward in retirement.

Tendulkar can now be seen as a foretelling of Indian success, on the field and off, by achieving when it was still uneven, uncertain, and unexpected. With a sense of that, he has discerned in the 2011 World Cup a special defining quality, the culmination, as it were, of a two-decade tournament: 'Nothing beats the World Cup final in 2011. That was the best cricketing day of my life.' Virat Kohl's tribute was so good it sounds apocryphal: 'Tendulkar has carried the burden of the nation for 21 years; It was time we carried him. Chak de India.' It is all the more meaningful for being true.

But with time, Tendulkar has also become the precious

property of his generation. In youthful India, celebrity is perishable; in modern India, heroes are plentiful. A demographic wave is being inducted in cricket with no direct memory of Tendulkar. They will, in due course, wonder how good he really could have been, whether their elders aren't just getting a little carried away. He'll increasingly be someone for those who saw him hold on to, to make claims for, to champion—what was true of The Master, Jack Hobbs, in John Arlott's poem, is no less true of The Little Master.

> The Master—records prove the title true,
> Yet fail you, for they cannot say
> How many men whose names you never knew
> Are proud to tell their sons they saw you play.

So 50, which we celebrate, while also knowing it will never be enough. Those who imagined that Bradman would surely live until the age of at least 99.94 will be loath to prophecy. But if ever a cricketer could be backed in pursuing a three-figure milestone by calm, courage and the studious husbandry of energy, it is Sachin Tendulkar.

INDRAJIT HAZRA

The greatest defender of fort and faith

Cricket, for me, is a bowler's game. The batter, at his or her best, defends the ramparts in front of which he or she stands, hoping to turn this defence of the fortress into a battle-winning counter-attack. In such a landscape, there is no greater defender of faith and fort than Sachin Tendulkar.

Tendulkar's ability to have not just played and dominated against the fiercest, cleverest attack, but to also have engaged willow to leather in such a way, with such consistency, with such *beauty*, is the mark of his genius. And in all his classical beauty of play is that unnatural poise of mind that he displayed pretty much from the first day he stepped on the international field in Karachi in 1989.

I saw Sachin first on TV, as most of us did then or in YouTube hindsight when he was 16 (and I, 18). Quite

The writer is a columnist and editor, sports, *The Economic Times*.

frankly, for the reasons mentioned above, I was more struck by Waqar Younis, who, along with Tendulkar, was making his international debut in the Karachi Test in November 1989. He had already scalped Sanjay Manjrekar and Manoj Prabhakar. Coming to bat at No. 6, what held my attention—and away from the Pakistani bowlers—was the cherub face under the white helmet managing to hold his ground at the National Stadium against the likes of Wasim Akram, Younis and Imran Khan.

This 'school boy' had come in to bat when India was reeling at 41/4. I had then figured that Sachin's youth alone to be his biggest virtue, the boy standing on the burning deck, etc. I followed the rest of the drawn Test mainly to see what Waqar would do after castling Tendulkar at 15 and picking up two more wickets in the first innings.

But how, over time, my attention shifted—not only to this calm figure in curls but to following Tendulkar as a talented youngster to one of the greats in the game, his age becoming more and more inconsequential. Over the years, both in the fag end of the 20th century and in the 2000s when Sachin took wing and how, he picked up traction, runs, of course, but also a grace in action that I have not seen before or after in a batsman.

There is enough evidence of Sachin's abilities charted through his career in innings and matches in all formats of the game. But greatness in a batsman being a composite of great moments of play; I need to share a few deeply

entrenched ones to showcase my understanding of his
superb art and craft. Treat it as a montage of strokes that
make not just Sachin's repertoire of shots but also what
makes him the player who *thinks up* such shots.

1998, 24 April, Sharjah, Coca-Cola final: India chasing
Australia's 272, Sachin is already on fire. With all that joyous
din from the stands, Shane Warne comes in to bowl in the
20th over—round the wicket. Sachin trips down the wicket
to meet the ball against the spin—it is a Bharat Natyam 1-2-3
step—and connects and hammers the ball over long on for
a six. This is not just power but also poise.

Nothing in cricket, and arguably nothing in sport,
match Tendulkar's on-drives. They are not drives but really
steers, directions, like Newtonian action more in the realm
of physics than in the 'physical' world. One such moment
(far too many) that I have seared in my memory bank is
against Sri Lanka in the 2011 World Cup in Mumbai. Nuwan
Kulasekara bowls one hurtler between the middle and leg
stump. Sachin steps forward to greet it, elbow up almost in
a namaste, were it not for his bat in hand. The bat is up as
a shield, Tendulkar lifting it just a little as if to shake a fly
off. The sheer timing of that straight drive is impeccable and
bisects the field as if by some surgical instrument. Tendulkar
scored 18 before departing, but who cares? After *that* shot, I
certainly didn't, I certainly don't.

And lest I be mistaken for someone who can't see the
grace in Tendulkar's power—or is it Tendulkar's power in

his grace—I have to recall that over boundary off Andrew Caddick in the 2003 World Cup match in Durban. Caddick's ball is short, wide of the off stump and ready for punishment. But what kind of punishment for the rising errant ball? Tendulkar swivels off the ball of his feet executing a pull shot that is a cricket version of the gallows. Such is the power behind the contact that the ball goes out of Kingsmead into the trees outside the ground. But again, Sachin makes the pull-shot look like a flick of the fingers. Which, in a way, it is.

It isn't kosher to compare apples with oranges, and certainly not two great practitioners and their practice of two different sports. But in one matter, Sachin Tendulkar and Lionel Messi share a common, rare-as-Kryptonite trait: their utter calmness, poise—for the lack of the perfect word, maturity—that has honed their skills to perfection. Without a doubt, this calmness of leela, even at his most blistering moments, marks Tendulkar out from the rest of the greats, making him, in my book, truly the greatest defender of the wicket—and cricketing faith.

NEERU BHATIA

Sachin Tendulkar @ 50

It was 1996. I was a rookie reporter then, wielding the mike with a leading Television network-TV Today; he was the young Team India captain. It was a one-off Test match in Delhi at the historic Feroz Shah Kotla versus Australia, led by their inspiring captain Mark Taylor. My brief, as given by my editor, was to ask the toughest question in the pre-match press conference—then a not so formal affair as it is these days. It was on the balcony, outside the old dressing rooms overlooking the wicket until the latter was shifted to a new building block square of the wicket. As soon as 'the Indian captain' stepped out to look at the Kotla pitch, I waved my mike in front of Tendulkar and asked him, 'Do you think the pressure of captaincy is affecting your batting?'

Neeru Bhatia is the Deputy Chief of Bureau-sports with *The Week* magazine.

He stopped in his tracks. I got a piercing look from the Indian captain, one that I can still remember starkly from an already declared great player, and responded thus: 'No, I don't think so.' Quietly said, politely yet firmly. And then he went on towards the centre wicket.

That, ladies and gentlemen, was my first direct interaction as a cricket reporter with Sachin Tendulkar, not the captain or Indian player but one of the greatest ever cricketers in the making. As things turned out, Tendulkar was removed as captain after a three-match drawn test series in Sri Lanka by the BCCI. Describing it as an 'unceremonious sacking' in his autobiography *Playing It My Way,* Tendulkar revealed that the dumping only made him more determined to become an even better cricketer.

And so, as the years passed, the Tendulkar legend grew more and more; the pleasure he gave to all cricket fans, players, teams, supporters, media, innumerable innings to go ga-ga over; I tend to believe with even greater certainty that I am glad to have been part of this glorious journey in my own little way. As time passed, the interactions have grown in number—lengthier, less abrupt, more one on ones—the comfort level getting better by the day; some on away tours—at wee hours in the morning in Sydney, for example, after the memorable 2003–04 Test series ended, at the TV studio after the recording of a programme by the official broadcasters, some at home in India.

There is no hiding from the fact that every time Sachin

went out to bat, he was followed by a million prayers and expectations. It was always the same since he made his mark on the world stage as a 16-year-old; as his stature grew, so also did the hopes of his billion Indian fans, who stayed glued to the TV sets till he was in the middle. I was no different, part of the 'Tendulkar generation', as I call it, the entire legion of fans that lived, laughed and cried every moment of his cricketing time. Even before I completed my postgraduate diploma course in mass communication and became a reporter in mainstream media, I, as a member of the 'Tendulkar generation', was as touched and affected by Tendulkar's cricketing exploits as the guy or girl next door. By the time he called time on his cricket career in 2013, as the one with 34,357 international runs to his name—at his home ground, the Wankhede stadium in Mumbai, as his voice choked with emotion during his farewell speech, time stood still as he spoke, the reporter took the back seat, and the Tendulkar fan came to the fore, memories of all the matches he played and won for Team India rushed forward. This farewell was like none I had witnessed or been part of till now, and there had been a few in my life journey till then.

In my journey of over 25 years as a sports reporter/writer, I have been lucky to have watched from the best seat in the stadium many a Tendulkar innings but perhaps the one that touched me the most was the one in the Sydney Test in 2003–04. It was an innings like none other of Tendulkar's. Devoid of any emotion, it was a meticulously crafted 436 ball, 241 not out made in 613 minutes or 10 hours and 21 minute long vigil. Not a single ball played on the up, each of his 33 fours hot on the ground, finding the gaps, beating the fielder. Not a single six in the innings. An exhibition of supreme control over his batting, pre-decided and pre-planned. Yes, it wasn't a display of exquisitely timed shot-making that has been so many of his ODI and Test innings; this was something else. A master playing his own way, batting on his own terms. The match and the series may have been drawn 1–1, but if anyone left an indelible stamp on it, it was Tendulkar.

Lastly, a request that I can never forget in my reporting life—as India reached the finals of the 2003 World Cup in South Africa, as the team geared up to meet Australia in the final match on an overcast day in Wanderers, Johannesburg, the delirium of seeing India reach its first WC final in 20 years reached South Africa too. As hordes of Indian cricket fans landed in Johannesburg the previous night or two before the final match, I called Sachin in his hotel room; I had to try there was no option. As I identified myself, he greeted me warmly. I requested him for an interview as my magazine was going to print before the final match. Could it be possible to talk to *The Week* about this World Cup, his thoughts, and his performances so far? His response was: 'Can we do this post the final if we win, please? You know how important this final match is for me, the team, you and all of us. It's more important to win than do an interview...'

he requested. He did not say outright no or yell at me for having the audacity to ask for one before the final. What could I say? I sighed deeply and said, 'Sachin, I understand... all the very best for the final,' and kept the phone down.

India was beaten resoundingly by Australia in the 2003 World Cup final, with Sachin scoring a mere four runs. Nobody talked after the match; nobody wanted to. It took another eight years to realise the dream of winning a World Cup for Sachin. But, perhaps, more than India winning it, the joy of seeing Sachin being part of a World Cup-winning team, after all, lifted on the shoulders by his younger teammates during the victory lap, that's my lasting memory. The happiness and joy on Tendulkar's face said it all. It was all worth it—the joy, the pain, the agony, injuries, string of wins, losses, runs made, runs missed. He was a part of us. Always will be.

G. RAJARAMAN

It is nearly a decade since he last walked out to bat in Indian colours. And yet, it's a good wager that when you recall any of Sachin Tendulkar's numerous knocks, even randomly, you simply can extend your hands and feel the electricity in the atmosphere even today.

Tendulkar's place in the pantheon of batsmen is above everyone else I have seen wield the willow. Of course, M.L. Jaisimha, G.R. Viswanath and Sunil Gavaskar were before my time as a sports writer, but I did get to watch Hyderabad's Mohammed Azharuddin and V.V.S. Laxman, Rahul Dravid, Sourav Ganguly, Virender Sehwag and, in the past decade, Virat Kohli have also enthralled one and all.

Even they will concede that Tendulkar was the one who walked in with the burden of expectation of a whole nation on his shoulders. No star's departure from the middle caused an exodus from the stands as his. No batsman had caused as many television and radio sets to be switched off when he was dismissed as he has. No cricketer has had such an effect on an entire population as he has.

Definitely not for as long.

Indeed, while no cricketer (and perhaps no sportsman) has had such a following as he has, it may seem quite far-fetched to correlate the growth trajectory of the Indian economy and his career with one another. Since his arrival on the international scene coincided with India opening its market, it will be fascinating to study their parallel journeys.

Just as some economists pointed out that the reforms began in the 80s and played a crucial role in stimulating growth during that decade, sports historians will place the 1983 Prudential Cup victory as the milestone moment in Indian cricket. But like the economic growth story, cricket development was intermittent, if not entirely fragile.

The liberalisation in the 90s was more systematic and systemic. The reforms in India's policy on deregulation of industry, external trade and liberalisation led to the opening of the economy and the parallels in his international cricketing career in the 24 years he proudly represented the country.

India's GDP in 1983 was assessed at $296.04 billion and rose to $1,856.72 billion in 2013, while the annual growth rate of GDP rose from -3.68 per cent in 1989 to 6.39 per cent in the year of his retirement from international cricket. Not for a moment am I suggesting that this was his doing, but the parallels cannot be missed as Indian cricket's stock rose on the world stage.

We can only hazard a guess about his immense

contribution to the overall image of the nation's cricket team and the nation itself as one of its finest ambassadors. But the truth is that he instilled greater faith in fellow Indians' minds with his feats on the cricket pitch. He may not have set out to do that deliberately, but it was a fantastic byproduct of his times as a cricketer.

It was just as well that Tendulkar's arrival on the scene also preceded the onset of cable and satellite TV in the early 1990s by a year-and-a-half, but it was almost as if he was warming up for its arrival. He was India's first mega sports star of the cable and satellite TV era, extending his run past the dawn of social media as well.

To his credit, he learnt quickly to come to terms with both the positive and negative spin-offs of being a leader in the climate of change that was sweeping India. An acute awareness of the potential and an urge to make the team express itself in much the same manner as himself endeared him to millions of Indians.

In many ways, Tendulkar's association with Mark Mascarenhas and WorldTel opened amazing possibilities for Indian cricketers. In 1995, he signed a Rs 45 crore deal with WorldTel, making many jaws drop in amazement. Of course, many cricketers had endorsed products before and had featured in commercials, but this deal blew everyone away.

He was not at the helm when the Indian cricket team courted success across formats, but he was a critical part of the machinery that woke up the sleeping giant and the think tank that chartered a path for India. When India was encouraging foreign investment, he was instrumental in getting New Zealander John Wright as the team coach.

Fans and some critics found it hard to accept Tendulkar's evolution (I use the word deliberately) to a more sedate, accumulator role post 1999. They would not consider that time has taken a toll on his body and that he had to contend with injuries to the back, heel and fingers and suffered a tennis elbow. But he remained a rock that the team would depend on.

To be sure, the Indian team's unexpected triumph in the inaugural ICC World Twenty20 in South Africa spurred the growth journey, hastening the arrival of the Indian Premier League. Of course, he was not part of the squad that won the crown in 2007, but he played no mean role in ensuring that the Indian sports entertainment industry was ready to welcome the new kid on the block.

The IPL economy has its own logic, quite different from all other representative cricket rakes in the moolah; be it the ICC events or the bilateral series that the Board of Control for Cricket in India. And he played no mean role in establishing its brand in its nascent years with his magnetic presence that made fans shed parochial feelings and cheer him even in his team's away matches.

Much later, some years after he put his cricket bats away, Tendulkar was a part of the movement that backed the return of Indian coaches, Ravi Shastri first and then Anil Kumble and now Rahul Dravid. In many ways, he was championing the cause of self-reliance long before the term *Atma Nirbharta* started to feature in our day-to-day conversations.

DEBASIS SEN

It was a memory of a lifetime with the master in Durban

Sachin Tendulkar is an emotion for each and every Indian. He evoked patriotism every time he walked into bat for India. There is no bigger sporting legend in India than the master blaster. There is no better sight than a packed cricket stadium cheering 'Sachin, Sachin'.

He made people cry when he got out and brought joy in the faces of millions when he scored a hundred. He had to be requested to pacify the angry Eden Gardens crowd after Shoaib Akhtar got him run out in the Asian Test Championship in February 1999; such was his image.

I remember bunking my classes to be at Eden Gardens to watch the Hero Cup semi-final and final to watch the legend, and he did not disappoint.

The first time I watched the master from close quarters was on the tour to Pakistan in 2005–06. The popularity Sachin shared across the border was simply incredible. Every time he walked into bat, fans in all the stadiums across Pakistan greeted him with loud cheers.

The best memory I shared on that one-and-a-half-month trip to Pakistan was when the master chose to spend time with the travelling Indian journalists at Multan airport. The Indian team flight was delayed by a couple of hours, and he took time for an informal chat with the touring Indian media. He also posed for a photograph with the journalists covering the tour.

The tour to South Africa in 2011 was the first time I had the opportunity to interview the master. It was a memorable tour as India drew the test series 1–1, but most importantly, Sachin scored his 50th Test hundred in the first test match at SuperSport Park in Centurion. He scored an unbeaten 111* on a lively track against Dale Steyn & co. The travelling Indian media contingent decided to felicitate him for the milestone, but he requested to keep it after the test series. He was not playing in the ODI series that followed. On Tuesday, 13 January 2011, the felicitation ceremony was fixed at the team hotel (Southern Sun Elangeni hotel) in Durban, the day before the ODI series began.

The master graciously agreed to be part of the small function in which he was presented with a vuvuzela, a cowboy hat, a book on Nelson Mandela, and an African wildlife plaque which had 50 inscribed on it. I had the honour, along with other colleagues, to present a Jabulani football (the official match ball of the 2010 FIFA World Cup) to the master. He cut a cake and opened a champagne bottle with us. It was a lifetime experience as the master spent almost an hour.

Sachin sir always had the utmost respect for the media. I still remember on the tour to England in 2011, during the Birmingham riots, he used to enquire about the safety of the touring media. The popularity master shared across the cricket world is unparalleled. And it is still the same.

Thanks for the happy memories, Sachin sir.

ABHIJIT SARKAR

I was an enthusiastic young executive in the prestigious Chairman's Office of Sahara in 1996 when I was assigned to invite and bring Sachin Tendulkar to the corporate exhibition set up in Mumbai. A 23-year-old Sachin had already created a mark on the global cricket map and stamped his greatness at that point.

I first met him when I went to pick him up. He was diligently changing the tyre of his car under the hawkish gaze of his elder brother, Ajit and Kiran More, who were teaching him this new skill. I learned that he had insisted on learning to change the stepney of the car. Once done, we went up to his flat and had litchi juice. Soon he was ready to leave, and he insisted I accompany him in his car. We picked up Raju Kulkarni on the way, and on reaching the exhibition site, he again prevailed upon me to accompany him throughout the visit. This first meeting was followed by a gradual build-up of the relationship when our paths crossed again at Sahara Cup in Toronto, where we got to know each other better.

There was also this historic assembly of the Indian and

Pakistan teams where I coordinated with the respective Boards to get them to stay in Sahara Shaher in Lucknow after playing in Kanpur in 2006. A massive live stage show was organised for a very private gathering with the teams where Shah Rukh Khan made the cricketers dance to his tunes, was organised. The players' banter amongst themselves, especially with Sachin, was heart-warming. Shoaib Akhter famously mentioned that he had picked up Sachin at 3 am and dropped him on the floor. Everyone may have heard of that incident, but very few would know it happened before my eyes in Lucknow.

I also distinctly remember when he was invited to the Sahara India Sports Awards in 2010 and it was Anjali's birthday. He received my call on the first ring when everyone failed to contact him to take his confirmation. He came despite his engagement and had a wonderful time at the event.

Being the legend that he was and is, he did not need to make me feel privileged on the numerous occasions that he did, whether it was a mention in his autobiography or calling me out from the stage during the Sports Awards or in the celebrations inside the dressing room following the historic World Cup win in 2011 or the numerous meetings that followed over the years. The celebrations after the World Cup 2011 win were made more momentous for me as I was on the team bus ride that night from the Wankhede to the hotel, where the party continued till 4 am.

He is and will indeed remain the most modest, humble achiever in modern times. Over the years, his hunger to learn, which I have witnessed, has enabled him to reach where he is.

SACHIN BAJAJ

Sachin Tendulkar symbolised the spirituality of cricket

What can you write about a man who has symbolised the hopes and aspirations of a nation on the biggest stage for over two decades? Sachin Tendulkar isn't a cricket player alone but an icon. Surely, you have heard that many times! It's been nearly a decade since he last played for India, but the power of his appeal continues to this day. People love him as much, if not more, as they did when he took India to glory. That is a mark of the legacy of the man!

In the 1980s, Sachin Tendulkar rang through the school cricket circuit in Mumbai (then Bombay). The plethora of big scores in the Giles and Harris Shield made the world take notice, none more than the epic partnership with his friend Vinod Kambli. However, I would go back to a time when the sheer precociousness of Sachin's talent made an institution change its rules.

The Cricket Club of India (CCI) often inducts promising

players into their teams to provide them with good exposure and fast-track their development. However, anyone under 18 couldn't enter the main clubhouse. In the past, young players had to walk in through the stands towards the field and be a part of the game. Hemant Kenkre, our cricket captain and the former Mumbai cricketer Milind Rege, spotted Sachin's precocious abilities. Madhav Apte, our then president, and Raj Singh Dungarpur took notice of Sachin's incredible talent and convinced the club's Executive Committee (EC) to make an exception for him. The rules were changed, and Sachin could enter the clubhouse and represent CCI. One must also remember that Sachin's introduction to the CCI had his guru Ramakant Achrekar's blessing. Only after his approval was it taken forward.

Sachin's first impression for the club remained etched in memory. We faced Rajasthan Sports Club in the Kanga League at the Brabourne Stadium. Sachin walked out to face Pradeep Sunderam, one of the best fast bowlers on the domestic circuit. The young Sachin smashed the first ball from a length over Sunderam's head and into the stands to showcase his arrival. Those who saw that still remember it because it showed that the youngster wouldn't get overawed by a bigger platform. That attitude carried on as he marked his Ranji debut with a century and later donned the Test cap on a challenging tour to Pakistan at the age of 16.

The statistics, records and achievements have been mentioned time and again. However, the man behind it all makes it more special. Despite being a star, he remained grounded and connected to his roots. Even after he started playing for India, he would turn up for CCI on numerous occasions—to give back to the club that supported him. He always mentioned Madhav sir and Raj sir's contributions to his cricketing career. His passion for the game remained the same until his last game, and it was motivational for the others around him.

His passion translated into a great work ethic—with him putting in the hard yards at practice. During his final years at the highest level, he would turn up at the CCI for practice. Usually, the practice would start at 10 am, but he would be in the dressing room at 8 am. He would clean his shoes, get his equipment ready and talk to the people around. He would chat with the groundsmen, dressing room attendants and everyone involved and connected with the game. He would try to know about their lives and contribution to the game.

That signalled a deep spiritual connection to the game of cricket. We treat cricket like a religion in India, and the cricket ground was a temple for Sachin. He symbolised the spirituality of the sport and carried forward the torch of the gentleman's game. At the CCI, we were blessed to have witnessed him grow from an early age.

As he completes another half century—we wish him good health, success and long life.

ROHIT BANSAL

That's Mr Tendulkar—for an ordinary devotee

The invitation to write in a Festschrift for Sachin Tendulkar sent me into a bout of 'who-am-I'. Especially after the historian co-editor, Dr Boria Majumdar casually shared the cast of 49 other contributors. What can one write that doyens of the game—each spoilt for choice in anecdotal material—wouldn't?

A few hours before the hard deadline, a little bird in my existentialist mind state finally whispers. Mine is a slot that the 'subaltern' editor would reserve for 'the ordinary devotee'. Aha! The penny has dropped. So, here goes.

I didn't know of Mr Tendulkar in his first few innings. In those days, an actor by the same first name (no surname) was known to more people. For a billion of us, 13 December

The writer is a former editor. He is presently a group leader at Reliance Industries Limited.

1989, was destined to change that. A Waqar Younus bouncer felled a cherubic 16-year-old son of middle-class India. This was war. The Pakistanis roared just as our hearts sank. My mind, I must confess, even flirted with the horrible idea if this were the end-of-story, a re-enactment of Nari Contractor falling to Charlie Griffith. A few seconds later, the bonding of a lifetime was destined to be. A boy had fallen. But it was Mr Tendulkar who got up. Legend has it that he defiantly whispered, "mein khelega". A favourite son was born. His 57 saved us the Test—and for me, that "mein khelega" meant moving mountains to tune in to nearly every inning the great man would play over the next 24 years. Oh, those eyes beneath the helmet with that little tricolour!

For my father, 50 years older and never a great one for following the game ball-by-ball, Mr Tendulkar's batting remained the exception even in the hospital bed.

Unlike millions, life has been good enough to afford me some meet-ups. Some were so short that Mr Tendulkar might need some help remembering them, but they always left me, 'the ordinary devotee', marvelling at how a man with God-like following can be so thoughtful. Being a monk is difficult when random people thrust cameras at you at every step. You have the family by your side, and people are rudely brushing past. Yet, have we heard of the man losing his shirt? That's Mr Tendulkar.

My favourite subaltern story is when we were onboard a commercial flight. Thanks to our common connection with Boria babu, Mr Tendulkar and I chatted briefly. Then the flight landed in Mumbai. I hit the sky bridge first. Behind me, I could sense that an entire entourage of ushers had surrounded Mr and Dr Anjali Tendulkar for selfies. Walking fast to avoid the melee, I gained over 50 metres lead. But what do I hear? The hooter of a golf buggy! I peer to my left, and who do I see? Mr Tendulkar smiled mischievously, signalling me to hop on even as a crowd scrammed to catch up! That's Mr Tendulkar!

Likewise, the time that the autobiography came out. I sent Boria babu a case of 24, hoping to gift whatever number returned with 'the' autograph. Just four days later, what do I see? Every single copy was signed with a blue and green felt pen, Boria babu assuring me that even the Tendulkar family has yet to be able to get signed copies they are planning to gift. The recipients I chose looked happy getting the book, but no sooner I said it was an inscribed copy, each one broke into a radiant smile. That's Mr Tendulkar!

Boria babu engineered yet another situation as only he could. At the launch of his magisterial volume on the Olympics, co-authored with Dr Nalin Mehta, he had Mr Tendulkar seated between me and the peerless Mr Abhinav Bindra, the first Indian to win an individual Olympic gold. I made a fun wager about how Mr Tendulkar will divide his time. Will he even care to engage with me, seated to his right? How wrong could I have been! Instead, he went out of his way to chit-chat and even tried to find common ground for us. That's Mr Tendulkar!

Despite 10 years away from international cricket, Mr Tendulkar continues to unite Indians eight and 80. Over to the next 50—inspirer, role model, gentleman.

Quotes

He has given so much for Indian cricket. As my son Akash says, he can tell his grandchildren that he saw Sachin bat, so we must be happy that we have seen him play in our era. The most memorable memory of Sachin for me would be that how he would always pack his kit, and would take care of it like his baby.

—Mrs Nita Ambani on Tendulkar
on the eve of his retirement

Sachin is a legend…he's sheer poetry in motion. What can one say about one of the greatest of all time.

—Sanjeev Goenka

Sachin is god where batsmanship is concerned.

—Sir Viv Richards in 2012

It's been almost a decade since you quit the sport. Players, fans already realising the achievements and standards you have set and how difficult it is to beat leave alone come close. Living legend in the house.

—Ravi Shastri on Sachin Tendulkar
while wishing him on his 49th birthday

Sachin Tendulkar is the perfect example of talent plus hard work. Sachin had so much talent, we hadn't seen it in anyone. He was born in an era where he knew how to score hundreds. Sachin's strength was par excellence and incomparable.

—Kapil Dev to ESPNcricinfo

In my life time being in and out of Indian Dressing Room in various capacities I have never seen a man half as patriotic as Sachin Tendulkar. He opens his bag and there is Ganpati and there is flag of India.

—Raj Singh Dungarpur in an interview

SANJIV NAVANGUL

Beyond boundaries

The 1990s—a time of VCRs, Walkmans and Maruti-800s.

It was the era where there was just one angry young man—the Big B.

It was also the time when India was beginning to open its doors to foreign investments, ushering in the reformative era of globalisation and liberalisation.

And while India's economic recovery began, it coincided with the era of one of India's greatest sportsmen—Sachin Ramesh Tendulkar. So, as destined, the Little Master remains a symbol of the rise of India—a new Corporate India, and for 24 years, perhaps, he did more than that and helped to inspire it.

Several major MNCs either ignored India or gave up, Coca-Cola, for example, disappeared in India in 1977 and re-appeared in 1993. Surely, one could drop a parallel to Indian cricket. We were being sidelined. And the time had surely come, so also the idea whose time has come to rewrite India's economic growth story. This was the backdrop and a stroke of destiny, whether or not asked for, but Tendulkar and his cricketing career inspired a new India.

A soft-spoken, middle-class Indian who would allow his game to speak, akin to a quiet India who allowed herself to grow, Tendulkar was undoubtedly popular and is ranked 2nd amongst the top 10 Great Indians after Gandhiji (placed higher than Nehru). He soon became the icon of success and enjoyed this with dignity. India's growth story is similar. The average growth has accelerated slowly but steadily across key sectors—agriculture, industry and services and stands at about 7 per cent since 2008–09. An increase in productivity, investments and consumption and exports brought growth with stability.

All these factors fuelled the growth of Corporate India further. Diversified businesses, increased partnerships, and most importantly risk-taking abilities of Indian firms grew manifold. The resilience was evident. Look at how Corporate India recovered from two major policy events—demonetisation and implementing the Goods and Services Tax (GST), an important indirect tax reform.

India's remarkable growth experience lends credence to its long-term growth story. So also, the relentless passion for cricket in India is an incredible indication of progress and harmony. Today we see a dream in the eyes of many teens to be the next Sachin or the next Dhoni of the country.

Sachin gave several young Indians hope. Acknowledged as the 'God of Cricket'— having compiled over 35,000 international runs—Sachin turns 50 on 24 April 2023. And while the world celebrates this with smiles and cheer, Tendulkar remains one of the few who brought a smile on the faces of his countrymen—young and old alike; an unadulterated smile; while he remained standing tall, taking his guard, having braved several bowling attacks and adversity on the field.

Mother India is proud of this Bharat Ratna. While she celebrates 75 years of independence, she ushers a breath of fresh air and hope for all her citizens. A hope of an Amrit Kaal, hope to dare and dare to dream. Aspirations are on the rise, and as Indians work towards fulfilling them, the Little Master, born in Dadar, Mumbai, is a symbol of daring to dream to many.

Today there is hope. And where there is hope, there is a will to change for the better.

Ala-re-ala, Hope ala!

SHYAM SRINIVASAN

Dear Sachin,

Happy 50th Birthday! Well, that's definitely not all that I want to say.

Exactly 25 years back, on your birthday, I watched you live in Sharjah as you scored your second ton in three days. It was difficult to wrap my head around what I saw in that stadium, one youngster stood ground like a knight fighting goliaths, and I knew I was watching a star who would soon be in the pantheon of legends. I don't remember when you were first hailed as the 'God of Cricket' but I knew after the match that the moniker was for a lifetime. Ever since I've been watching, from a non-striker's end, all your duels.

Every match that we see is in the physical context. But there must have been so much going on mentally. Before, during, after the match and as you tour in return of their visit, nothing is conclusive. I've seen that while there is respect among the players, there is also fierce desire to win. While many got into slugfests which have had their own expiry dates, you have never been someone to chest thump, we have only ever seen a composed Sachin. Many a time, even when the decision was not in your favour, I don't recall any 'pitch-rage' . You just walked, maybe made a point or two. You were absolutely sure of how you wouldn't want to conduct yourself. Staying unfazed is a take-way for all of us. Why expend emotions when the media and the medium have eternal memory. When I look back at your conduct on and off-field, I think you just strode down with grace and humility. Sachin, you've shown us what it means to be a true leader, to inspire others through your actions, and to always stay true to your values. You have taught us that sometimes it's important for us to tuck our bat and simply walk away, knowing that we will be back.

Over the years you became a legend from a prodigy, saw the game change and even changed the game! A memorable innings which probably demonstrated to us all that the playbook can always be rewritten, was your 200* against the Proteas in Gwalior. Everyone finally believed that every impossible can be reached and breached. Cricinfo, the website, had crashed when you were on 198* as 5.5 million people had logged in to see the first double ton in history. And while you turn 50 you still hold the highest number of half centuries—264, a record which probably be never broken. The sheer longevity of your career offers a deep insight about how incredibly and maniacally focused you were about each innings of yours. This passion is a lesson in endurance for every soul, whether they follow or don't follow the game—stay long at the crease and things will happen. And I genuinely believe Sir Viv had the comment that explains you the best: 'He has been a genius when it comes to ability, a Trojan when it comes to work ethic and manic when it comes to his focus.' Neither did a bloodied nose stop you, nor did the tennis elbow. Both were impactful injuries and could have changed the course of your career. There surely are many more, but these two stand out, since you must have taken a step back, rethought of your strategy and made a significant comeback. Through your resilience you've inspired generations to chase their dreams and to never give up, and for that, we can't thank you enough!

How can I write about you and not mention the teary-eyed innings you played after the Mumbai siege. It was a moment that changed the country's sentiments and brought people together in a way that few other things could. Life as we know cannot be lived backwards but our memories make up for such moments which we want to re-live. We have memories, we all do—individually, with friends and families; but if we ask every Indian of a marquee memory they have, which overlaps with a billion more—only one name would emerge and that is yours! You were the link which gave a billion souls moments in their lives and a hope that India can never lose with Number 10 at the crease. And when Anjali said, 'I can imagine cricket without Sachin, but I can't imagine Sachin without cricket,'—neither could

I. But then I see your videos when you step out of your car and play some galli-cricket and spending a lot more time on things you love doing—family, travel, and so much more, I realize that from the maidans of Mumbai to a global icon, nothing changed the humble Sachin Tendulkar. Only your immeasurable love for the sport changed the sport immeasurably!

Batting at the crease and taking fresh guard:

S.R. Tendulkar – 50* | India – 75*

This is once in a life-time score. Wishing you the best for your chase of the next 50*.

Sachinists

SUDHIR GAUTAM

I have been a fan of Sachin sir since I was in class 5. I developed an interest in cricket watching him. I used to play cricket in school and, later on in life, also got selected for LS College in an Inter College tournament. But I was never allowed to play, and our games teacher ridiculed me once by asking me to go and meet Sachin sir if I was a diehard fan. He had no idea what Sachin sir meant to me and, in fact, had done me a favour. In 2002 I first saw Master playing an ODI against West Indies at the Keenan stadium in Jamshedpur. I still remember I went to Jamshedpur riding my bicycle. Thereafter I saw him playing an ODI at Eden Gardens on 19 January 2002 against England. I watched the fourth ODI at Green Park in Kanpur on 28 January in that same series. My journey with Sachin sir had started.

First meeting with Master

I went to Mumbai to watch the fourth ODI at the Wankhede stadium during the TVS Cup (tri-series involving India, New

Zealand and Australia from 23 October–18 November 2003).
I met him for the first time at Trident Hotel. He asked me to
visit his house. I was allowed inside and given juice to drink.
He gave me a jersey and a ticket to watch the match. It was
a dream come true for me. Before I left his house, he asked
me whether I wanted to watch more matches.

I jumped onto the ground and touched his feet in the
next match against New Zealand in Cuttack on 6 November
2003. Security immediately rushed inside and caught me.
Sachin sir told the security guys not to beat me and let me
go.

I went to Bangalore to watch the next match against
Australia at the Chinnaswamy stadium. But I could not
meet him. Sachin sir scored a century in the next game
against New Zealand at the Lal Bahadur Shastri stadium on
15 November. I thought India had lost the game the last
time I met him. But this time, not only was India on the
verge of winning the game, but he also scored a hundred.
So I jumped again and ran into the ground to meet him. The
police took me to the Secunderabad PS and gave me a good
thrashing before releasing me at night. I could not attend the
final at Eden Gardens, in which India lost.

I went to Mumbai and met sir again at his house. He
scolded me and said not to jump onto the ground again.
The only time I jumped again was in 2010 when Harbhajan
Singh scored a century against New Zealand in Ahmedabad.

Body painting and writing Tendulkar 10

I used to have hair during my student life. Then during my first visit to Jamshedpur, I bumped into Saroon Sharma. He had a map of India designed on his head while keeping his hair. So I decided to do the opposite, shaved the hair off but kept the design of the India map and had it painted. And when I first visited Mumbai on my bicycle to meet the Master, I had my body painted and written Tendulkar 10. I used to have it written only on the back, but after 2006 I also started writing it in front. I have kept the design of the India map since then, and it has become my identity.

Invited to the Indian dressing room after the 2011 World Cup win at Wankhede stadium

There was a campaign—Sachin ka sapna, World Cup hain apna. Sachin sir had previously participated in six World Cups but failed to win them. So, the sponsors had a campaign since it was his last World Cup.

After we lifted the World Cup on 2 April 2011 at the Wankhede stadium, security guys came to me in the stands. I started wondering what had happened as I had done nothing wrong. The security people took me towards the dressing room, where I saw Sachin sir signalling me to climb up. I could not believe it as I jumped three steps at a time to reach the dressing room.

I cannot describe that moment. I have to spend hours

painting my body as it needs to dry. At times I did not have food as well. I have been waving the tricolour and blowing the sankh because of my passion and love for Sachin sir. Zaheer (Khan) bhai told me to lift the World Cup trophy. Then Master called and clicked a photograph with me and the World Cup trophy. It could only happen because of Sachin sir.

Cheering Master during Road Safety Series

It has been nine years now since Sachin sir retired from international cricket. But he has not retired from my heart. Will never do. Sudhir Gautam is known as Sachin's fan. That's my identity. How can he ever retire? When he plays the Road Safety Series, I go and cheer him. He led the team twice to win the trophy. On both occasions, I was fortunate that he allowed me to hold the trophy and take a picture with him. After he retired from International Cricket, I started writing Miss U Tendulkar.

Sponsoring overseas trips to cheer the Indian team

I met him and expressed my desire to cheer the Indian team during the 2015 World Cup in Australia. He did not hesitate as he organized my flight tickets, hotel bookings and visa. He even wrote to the Embassy so that I do not face any trouble.

I still remember I reached Adelaide on 14 February, a day ahead of India's opening fixture against Pakistan. I was disappointed I was not allowed to go near the practice arena.

He ensured that I was cheering the team during practice sessions from the next match.

He has organized my tickets and visa whenever I have travelled outside India. He also arranged my recent visit to Australia for the 2022 T20 World Cup.

Visiting Sachin sir's house on his birthday

I feel very happy whenever I visit his house on his birthday. He cuts a cake with his fans, and it makes our day. I have been carrying paintings, Ganesh's idol, Ramakant Achrekar sir's painting, for him on his birthdays. Last two years, he did not celebrate his birthday with fans because of COVID, and we look forward to returning this year. On most occasions, Mumbai Indians had an IPL match on Sachin sir's birthday at Wankhede stadium. Sir also gives me a ticket to watch the match in the evening.

Wishing Master on his 50th birthday

For me, Sachin Tendulkar is God, and I want to wish him a Happy 50th birthday. Furthermore, on behalf of all his fans, I wish him the best year ahead.

PAWAN KUMAR

'Commit your crime when Sachin is batting because even God is watching him bat.'

Life was straightforward. Cricket was the priority, and everything else served as a filler between cricket matches. A 10-year-old is always searching for a superhero. Sachin was that superhero for me.

A country of billion plus would switch on their televisions and switch off their lives to watch him bat. He seldom disappointed them, singlehandedly knocking the mightiest of opponents down.

Do you think it was just cricket? It was the collective pride of India on display. Those were the times when a raised finger could break a billion hearts, and a raised willow could make them swell with pride! He has flooded my life with innumerable reasons to celebrate. Going to bed crying without food after Sachin got out became a daily routine.

He might not be playing today but watching him walk out to open the batting for India remains my favourite childhood memory. From his batting style to even the habit of chewing nails, we imitated everything. I might have grown old, but every time I see him, that little fanboy springs back to life.

The first time I watched Sachin play live was against Australia. When I reached the stadium, Australia was batting. The time finally arrived, and Sachin came in to bat. Chants reverberated all round. Sachin!!! Sachin!!! Sachin!!! I froze, and someone had to pinch me to bring me back to life. This was the beginning, and I promised myself this would only get bigger and better.

The first time I met, Sachin was an experience in itself. It was at 5:05 on 22 August when I first saw him. I wanted to go and say 'Hi!' and tell him what he meant to me. While I was darting towards him, I kept reminding myself to hold on to my emotions! I am getting extremely emotional while writing this. Finally, I told him, 'Sir, may I please have one snap with you? I am crazy about you,' and showed him my tattoo. On seeing the tattoo, his reaction was to be captured as he said, 'Whoa!!!'

The humble man that he is, he clicked a picture with me. I thanked Sachin for being so modest! Meanwhile, I asked if he liked the tattoo. He smiled and said, 'Yes.'

I have met him several times since then, but the first will always be special. I still cannot get enough of it!!!

TRISHA GHOSAL

I don't recall how and why I became a Sachin Tendulkar fan. But growing up, Sachin Tendulkar became synonymous with God for me. I had numerous scrapbooks, newspaper cuttings, and Boomer cards; everything was about the Master. But, I had obviously never imagined that I would be writing in a book dedicated to him.

I had Sachin's poster on my cupboard, and I would go to that poster for all sorts of help; I would pray in front of the poster even before my school exams. That's how much he means to me.

In 1996, I was on a train from Berhampore to Kolkata. At that time, Sachin was the team captain, which didn't go well with many people. I was just six years old and sitting with Sachin cards in my hand. Then, two men started criticising Sachin. I was tiny back then but left no stone unturned in standing up for my God. I screamed, I shouted, and I told them off eventually.

On 31 May 1998, I met Sachin Tendulkar for the first

time. It was the final of the triangular series between India, Kenya and Bangladesh at the Eden Gardens. Kenya won the toss and elected to bat first. They were bowled out for 196. While Kenya was batting, Tendulkar came and stood at the long-on boundary. I couldn't believe he was just a few feet away from me. I ran towards the nets like all the other spectators. He was so kind and humble and greeted everyone between balls. I kept screaming, but I was just a kid and thought my voice would never reach him. But to my astonishment, it did, and he turned, smiled and waved. That's it! My day, my match, everything was made. I was ecstatic for the rest of the game and the rest of the month. If only we had cameras back then.

I met him virtually a couple of times after the pandemic for interviews; I was at Eden Gardens (crying my heart out) for his penultimate test. But I can never forget 1998.

Each time I have been in awe of his humility. Sachin Tendulkar is not my God for the 100 hundreds or any other cricketing achievements; he is my God because he taught me the meaning of following one's dream. He taught me the importance of grit, passion, perseverance and hard work. So on his 50th birthday, I would like to pray to God to keep my God happy and healthy forever.

Ajit Tendulkar,
the Mentor

AJIT TENDULKAR

Did I ever imagine that Sachin would be one of the best cricketers ever? That he will score 100 international centuries and be a part of the World Cup winning team? Not really. All I had thought of was he would be a good batter. Though we wished, we did not start on a journey thinking he would play Test cricket. For us, it was one step at a time. The first step was to qualify for the Mumbai Under-15 team and various junior-level cricket tournaments, then the Ranji Trophy, before finally playing for India.

In our society, we have played a lot of cricket. I also used to watch from my balcony; many juniors played cricket. Sachin would be one of them, and he stood out in how he was playing. For me, it wasn't about technique at such a young age. His relaxed hands, the swing of his bat and the ball connection were excellent. I thought this talent should be nurtured. I had played some cricket and was confident that Sachin could become a good cricketer with proper coaching and guidance.

That's when I decided to take him to Ramakant Achrekar sir. Many have asked me, why Achrekar sir? Achrekar sir was the coach of Sharadashram, a school winning several cricket tournaments. Some of his players were doing exceptionally well in school cricket. My school, Balmohan, practised 70–80 metres away from Sharadashram's nets at Shivaji Park. As I transitioned from school to college, sir's students Chandrakant Pandit, Lalchand Rajput and Subhash Kshirsagar all happened to be my teammates. Chandrakant Pandit and Lalchand Rajput went on to play Test cricket for India. Subhash Kshirsagar played for Mumbai in the Ranji Trophy. As I spent time with them, I got to know more and more about Achrekar sir.

One incident remains etched in my memory. Despite our team's batters doing well in the middle, Chandrakant Pandit was still restless for his turn to bat. While few of us wanted to take time to settle in, Achrekar sir's students were raring to score from the very first ball. Their confidence level was different. I realised that though the distance between my school nets and Sharadashram nets was hardly 70–80 metres, the gap in mindset was huge. In my school nets, we would still discuss academics, whereas Achrekar sir's students would only discuss cricket. Some of my other friends were also playing for Achrekar sir's clubs in different divisions. All of this had made a perfect set-up which increased my conviction that Sachin should be under the tutelage of Achrekar sir, playing for Sharadashram.

As Sachin started playing for Sharadashram school and various club teams, very soon, he was able to impress everyone with his batting abilities and performances. sir also wanted to push the bar higher by exposing him to bowlers who were much senior in age, experience and quality. Some of them were even first-class level bowlers who were reasonably quick. Soon, at the age of 16, Sachin was in the Indian team, which toured Pakistan in 1989. After the first two Tests, I went to Pakistan to watch him play. My elder brother Nitin first suggested I go there to be with Sachin since he was too young and in a foreign land.

In the last Test match of the series at Sialkot, Sachin got hit on his nose. I had heard the sound of the ball hitting his helmet flap and nose and could see he was bleeding. But somehow, I felt he would continue. Even before his debut, Sachin had already got a taste of the challenges he would face if he was to play Test cricket. He loved taking responsibility; going off at that point would mean putting the team in trouble. I was sure he wouldn't do that. And it so happened that he decided to continue. What went unnoticed was that he was still not wearing a visor when he decided to continue. It meant he could again get hit on the same spot. But that's how he was. Sachin was never scared of getting hit by the ball. The pain did not seem to divert him from his responsibilities towards his team. During the tea break in that Test match, I remember going up to him to check on him. I could see a tape around his nose, and all I said was, 'It's okay, carry on.' He didn't really seem fussed.

Now that he is done with his career, I feel good mainly about two things. Firstly, very rarely do you see a cricketer admired by both—purists, who look at the technical aspects of batting and fans, who look at how exciting batting is. Sachin, fortunately, was admired by purists and fans alike. Most found his style of cricket attractive. And they loved watching him play.

The second thing was his ability to look for playing a variety of shots, experimenting with bowling and keep on improving. The type of deliveries which had hit his body during the tour of Pakistan was later dispatched for sixes. Regardless of his success, he stopped learning at no point in his career. When he was playing, we would discuss the game almost daily. He would always try and get better. Even if he had scored a hundred or a double hundred, the urge to get better had not diminished. Sachin has remained a student of the game forever, and that continues to stand out for me.

As I said at the start of this piece, I have to confess I never imagined he would score 100 international centuries. Numbers and statistics were not something we were after. He hadn't set out to score 35,000 international runs. It was all about trying to be the best version of himself, be a good batsman, and score as many runs as possible for the team. Being able to stay focussed has yielded him good results.

I wish him a very happy 50th birthday!

Acknowledgements

A very sincere thanks to Anjali, Ajit and the family for all their help. To Sukumar for the pictures.

To every contributor who made this tribute possible.

To Rahul and Sayantan at Simon and Schuster who have repeatedly said let's make this really special.

Finally, to every Sachin fan who will wish the master on his birthday and make this effort worth it.